SURVIVING A CYBERSTALKER

SURVIVING A CYBERSTALKER

HOW TO PREVENT AND SURVIVE
CYBERABUSE AND STALKING

ALEXIS MOORE

Ordering Information:

Quantity sales. Special discounts are available on quantity purchases by corporations, associations, and others. For details, contact the "Special Sales Department" at the address above.

Nothing in this book is meant to be interpreted as legal advice or the creation of an attorney-client relationship. Please consult with an attorney licensed in your state.

Table of Contents

Time is a precious gift. May this book help you defend and overcome cyberabuse and stalking, as it took precious time away from me.

Alexis Moore

Introduction

If you picked up this book, you're likely dealing with cyberabuse or stalking, or you are hoping to protect yourself from falling victim. If so, you are not alone! Millions experience cyberabuse and stalking around the world. The National Center for Victims of Crime (NCVC) reports that 6.6 million people experience stalking in one year in the United States alone. One in six women and one in 19 men have experienced stalking victimization at some point during their lifetime in which they felt very fearful or believed that they or someone close to them would be harmed or killed.

I think these numbers are just "the tip of the iceberg." These statistics don't include instances of cyberabuse. Further, there are many victimized by cyberabuse and stalking that never get through to a reporting agency because they are either ignored altogether or feel so abandoned and ashamed they do not report at all. My goal is to help change that.

Today predators continue to outpace law enforcement, legislative efforts, and victim resources because technology evolves so quickly that literally in a "blink of an eye" a predator has a brand new gadget. They have latest and greatest "cyber- tools" available to all the masses and are now using them to take heartless aim of victims, all with the "click of a mouse" or "the tap of their thumbs." The net has created a whole new playing field for predators. They use this tool to take the life out of a person within seconds, without inflicting any physical wounds and often without leaving a trace of evidence behind.

The goal of this book is to help educate, empower, and inform readers worldwide of the realities faced by victims. Moreover, the intent is to teach how to defend against cyberabuse and stalking by using the tools that are available today. I also share some "creative tactics" that I learned from my struggles overcoming cyberabuse and stalking, in hopes of helping others going through the same issues.

Many victims find little or no help from any law enforcement agency or victim service providers, even though there are stalking and cyberabuse laws. Regulations fail to evolve quickly enough to address the creativity and spontaneity of today's predators.

This book is written to help you protect yourself from cyberabuse and stalking and to empower you to fight back. It is vital to regaining control over your life in case you and a cyberpredator or stalker ever cross paths.

CHAPTER 1

Why I Wrote This Book

Just when I thought my life was "over," is when my life had just begun. But I didn't know this.

Like millions who have experienced domestic violence, I never imagined I would be "that" person. I also never thought I would be writing a book labeled as the foremost expert in the field of cyberabuse and stalking, but here I am.

Looking back on the day when I first reported instances of cyberstalking back in 2004, and long before it was a household name as it is today, law enforcement told me I was "crazy." After experiencing hundreds of incidents of cyberabuse and stalking, I was asked to stop reporting them. I thought my life was over... little did I know it was just beginning.

I truly believed that I was going to be living on the run, always looking over my shoulder, wearing my tennis shoes and jogging suit to bed for the rest of my life.

I am not going to sugar coat things; it wasn't easy getting here. Learning how to defend myself alone, without the support of anyone, except for my grandmother, was traumatic. So much so that at times I was so depressed that I even attempted to take my life.
I learned a hard life lesson, which was to value time more than anything and to value the miracle of life.

From the first time I reported cyberstalking and stalking incidents, my grandmother only had 20 months left to live. I didn't know that she didn't know that, but it turned out this way, and, for a valuable reason.

She told me that my story was going to have a happy ending and that because I was experiencing all of this hell that somehow, someway it was going to help shape my life and the lives of others for the better. She said that my overcoming all of the torture I was enduring was going to give me a special gift and that I just didn't know it yet.

I didn't find this very soothing back then, in fact, I thought my grandmother's pain meds were taking over the words she was speaking. Today, however all of these years later, I understand. The biggest gift that I received is that I now understand the gift of time and how precious it is and that it should not be taken for granted.

I didn't know that my grandmother only had 20 months left to live when I escaped the abusive relationship I was in. And it was not until many months after I first reported instances of cyberstalking and stalking to law enforcement that I began to realize how precious time was.

I thought physically separating from an abusive intimate partner and leaving everything behind that I held dear, was all it was going to take to be free. I thought that I would have plenty of time with her to enjoy the new found freedom that I had...free from domestic violence and emotional abuse. I was so wrong!

Time is something that we can never get back. It's gone with every passing second of every passing day. I wrote this book so that you won't have to lose as much precious time as I did. I have also written this book so that no one will ever be alone, without the support of an advocate, as I was throughout my battles overcoming cyberstalking and stalking.

Learning how to defend and overcome cyberabuse and stalking is the gift I want to share. Our lives should not be spent living or working in fear!

When I began writing the first edition of this book, I became the founder of an all volunteer non-profit crime victim advocacy organization, **Survivors in Action** in 2007, to help other abuse victims including those who have experienced cyberabuse and stalking.

I have spent countless hours as a volunteer advocate providing direct support to victims and their families from around the globe who have experienced stalking and cyberabuse. In addition to working with victims, I have interacted with convicted cyberstalkers and stalkers... the predators themselves. The interactions I had with them helped me to be better understand the mindset of the perpetrators. I did this so that I can educate, empower, and inform the public on how to defend against an attack. I also did it to help aid victims to become survivors more quickly. The time I lost years ago, I will never get back, but I can help you keep from losing it.

I am sharing with you examples of a predator's behaviors and how to defend and overcome instances of cyberabuse and stalking. The objective is to save you not only time but the horrible waste of living or working in fear!

CHAPTER 2

What is Cyberstalking?

What is cyberstalking?

Answer: Cyberstalking is a technologically-based "attack" on one person who has been targeted specifically for that attack for reasons of anger, revenge or control.

Cyberstalking can take many forms, including harassment, embarrassment, and humiliation of the victim. These incorporate emptying of bank accounts or other economic control such as ruining the victim's credit score, harassing family, friends, and employers to isolate the victim and using scare tactics to instill fear and more.

The term can also apply to a "traditional" stalker who uses technology to trace and locate their victim and their movements more easily (e.g. using Facebook notifications to know what party they are attending).

A true cyberstalker's intent is to harm their intended victim using the anonymity and untraceable distance of technology. In many situations, the victims never discover the identity of the cyberstalkers who hurt them, despite their lives being completely upended by the perpetrator.

Cyberstalking is not identity theft. An identity thief, whether stealing from a stranger or a family member, has a very specific goal in mind — financial gain. Identity thieves are unconcerned by the consequences of their behavior on the victim's life, whereas the actions of a cyberstalker are deliberate and focused on the consequences to the victim.

Why the label "Cyberabuse":

Predator's use of technology to stalk continues to outpace law enforcement, victim resources and – legislation. The label "cyberabuse" has evolved to become the general term utilized as the umbrella to encompass all cyber- related conduct that is being perpetrated by predators online.

Examples of cyberabuse are:

- Cyberstalking
- Cyberbullying
- Non-consensual pornography
- Revenge porn
- Cyberrevenge
- Cyberattacks
- Stealthing
- Identity theft as abuse
- Email attacks and email bombs
- Spoofing
- Sextortion
- Email forgery
- Online impersonation
- Online misinformation and defamation

- Hacking and computer control
- Keylogging
- and whatever new conduct "predators discover to practice

CHAPTER 3

I Was a Victim of Cyberstalking

I was doing regular errands when I got the first sign that I wasn't free of a bad relationship. I soon learned that I would be further controlled and humiliated.

At that first moment, I didn't know just how devastating or lengthy my ordeal would be. I just knew something had gone very, very wrong.

Standing at the main gas station in our small town, I swiped my credit card and put my hand on the pump handle, ready to lift it up when the payment went through. Nothing happened. I tried again. This time a note flashed on the electronic board, "Please see the cashier." I ignored the message and tried another credit card instead. Crap. Same message: "Please see the cashier." WHAT WAS THE HELL GOING ON?

My heart was pounding, the way it does when you know, you might be in trouble, but you don't know what or why. Could it have something to do with my recent change of address? I'd left an abusive relationship a few short weeks before. It didn't occur to me to connect my problem to this escape. It must be a mistake. I knew that I had money in my bank account, so whatever was happening with the credit cards could be dealt with later.

The ATM card didn't work either. Worse yet, it said there were "insufficient funds." I leaned back on the gas pump feeling faint as if all the blood in my body had stopped moving. Where was my money?

When I finally got home and checked into it, I realized that someone had closed all my credit cards, transferred money out of my bank account, and all the credit card companies and banks were insisting I had done it.

"Alexis, you faxed us yourself with the request," the faceless credit card people said to me, implying in their tone, and occasionally in words, "Are you that stupid?"

TARGETED BY A CYBERSTALKER

I still didn't put together that I was being targeted by someone with malicious intent until other distressing things happened. Over the course of the next few months, in addition to the canceled credit cards and stolen money, my medical and car insurance were cut off, my credit rating plummeted, and process servers came after me on false claims.

There was only one person with enough information about me and knowledge of how to work the system to do this: my ex. I had a worst-case scenario cyberstalker — a predator who knew all my passwords, addresses, birthdate, mother's maiden name
– all the personal stuff that makes up our technological identity. He was determined to use all of his knowledge against me and became the worst kind of cyberstalker; persistent, well-informed and malicious.

I lost the ability to work. I lost my money and, even worse, my good credit history, which meant I couldn't move, get an apartment, get a car, get a loan or find a job. I lost friends and the support of family. And after two solid years of torture and abuse, there was even a point when I lost the will to live.

After reporting incidents of cyberstalking and stalking to law enforcement, I knew right away; they were not taking me seriously. They told me that I was crazy and to stop reporting altogether.   I refused! It wasn't easy to stand up for myself, my entire life was crumbling apart piece by piece, and I was not feeling confident, but that sick sense inside of me kept telling me to report, document and never back down or I would be living this life for the rest of my life. I didn't want to be a victim. I wanted to get this "shit" dealt with and put behind me. I was exhausted, and my life was being taken away from me electronically. I wasn't going to lie down and let it just "happen." I refused to be a victim. I didn't want my newfound freedom from an abusive relationship to now be completely engulfed with abuse all over again! I wanted my life back!

This mindset was one that began to take hold early on. Thanks to my grandmother's love and support of me and, because she was also targeted and viciously stalked and cyberstalked, it propelled me to take hold and continue to evolve. My grandmother was 81 years old and willing to fight back, and I would be damned if I didn't fight back too!

I still remember breaking down on her sofa where I sunk deep into the cushions and asked, "Nani, how am I going to make it through all of this? The cops don't believe me, the DA won't do anything, and my entire life is upside down, and so is yours! This can't go on forever, can it?"

Although she didn't have the solution, her support and telling me not to back down, to fight and refuse to be a victim is what lit that fire that was deep within my soul. My soul and spirit had broken, but it was beginning to light up again.

My "spirit furnace" hadn't fully been lit up until the day came when I was told "not to report anymore," and that I was "crazy" by a sheriff's deputy. I won't ever forget it, and I am grateful for the experience now more than ever!

If it had not been for this deputy calling me "crazy" and telling me not to report instances of stalking, and what is now called "cyberstalking" again, I would not be here as the strong advocate that I am. I am a "Survivor In Action." I probably wouldn't have passed the California bar the first time, nor achieved half the goals I set out to do back then.

There is no disdain here, except for the fact that I lost precious time. Yes, indeed for that I do remain "angry" as well steadfast in my goal of ensuring others don't lose the time as I did.

What it takes:

I am not going to tell you "BS." There is no easy way about it. Being stalked or experiencing cyberstalking or any form of cyberabuse is horrible...devastating in fact. Trying to defend against it and overcome it, is even worse.

Here's why:

There are no direct support services in the United States (or other countries) for victims. There are plenty of hotlines and so-called victim resources:

- National Stalking Resource Center
- National Network to End Domestic Violence
- Office of Victims of Crime
- National Coalition Against Domestic Violence
- National Crime Victim Bar

The list goes on and on and on and on (this is purposeful, to show the number of agencies, and yet no direct support for victims) and most are government funded. But once you reach out for direct support and are looking for "help" in the form of direct support to overcome and defend there is no help

I like to "prove" this by calling hotlines on behalf of victims and send emails out to them, requesting help from these so-called victim service providers. I provide the responses that come from these so called "victim service providers" as "proof" to public officials or naysayers when they doubt what I am saying is true.

It is true. Trust me, I lived it and continued to help others because there is no help anywhere else!

Other than a handful of underfunded grass roots organizations like the one I founded (Survivors in Action), there is no help. Defending and overcoming becomes even more problematic for victims, and in turn, fuels the ability of the predator to wreak havoc and destroy people's lives. It also takes away precious time.

I was all alone, and worse yet, being told not to report to the police. Then, I learned that my time with my sole supporter, my grandmother, was running out. The odds were stacked against me quickly, but I kept going.

My grandmother was diagnosed with cancer just a few months after I first experienced and reported the incidents of cyberabuse and stalking, to the authorities. Little did I know I would soon be fighting this battle alone.

I didn't know that I only had 20 months left with my grandmother back then. If I would have known, I am not sure if I would have done anything differently, but I can assure you that losing that precious time I had with her, fighting against a stalker and a vicious cyberpredator lit a fire in me that will never burn out! This flame is on fire, and I won't quit until the work is complete!

I lost that precious time, and I vowed then, and I continue to keep my vow today. I made a sacred promise to my late grandmother and myself that I would never back down, or be quiet again. I lost precious time, in fact, I wasted time, while I invented the wheel on how to overcome and defend cyberabuse and stalking.

For you the readers, I wrote this book for one reason. To help you save time and get your life back faster. Because wasting time combating cyberabuse and stalking is nothing anyone should have to endure, much less alone as I was back in 2004.

This book does not provide any legal advice. I am not creating an attorney-client relationship. I am not an expert at anything. The media and society like "labels." Cute ones even like "cyberharasser" and "stealthing." Sick as it all is, these labels are the only way that positive social change will happen. A label is a headline and a way to keep the topic active on a search engine. Therefore, I/we survivors use the tools that we have, and keep it "real."

The need for labels became clear to me right away because no one knew what the hell cyberstalking was when I reported it back in 2004. I had no name for it either. I said, "I am being stalked electronically, please help me!"

"Stalked electronically" was not a good label then and, because cyberstalking didn't obviously fit within any label, I was shit out of luck. The real SOL!

It wasn't identity theft either. I will be damned if law enforcement and everyone that I reported to, or described incidents too (that didn't think I was crazy of course), didn't want to put it in that "tidy box" and give it the label "identity theft," and then send me packing. "Lady you are a victim of identity theft. There is no help here unless your case involves a financial loss of $50,000 or more".
Today, I have plenty to say in response to this issue of the $50,000 loss!

"No sir, no madam, my loss is not $50,000, but my life and the precious time I lost is priceless!" I am fighting back and will never back down.

I had to help make the cyberstalking label "happen." I had to push to create this "label," defining it because the media likes labels, and so do public officials. Laws won't evolve, and more victims would be left behind just like me.

Also, the media likes credentials for their sources, and we need media to bring about awareness and awareness is what it takes to bring about positive social change. I, in turn, became a "cyberstalking expert," "victim," "author," "survivor," "advocate." It doesn't matter to me what label I have, so long as the information regarding cyberstalking is taken note of, so others like myself will no longer suffer the destructive consequences of such hatred.

Back then I didn't give a shit about how I was labeled nor do I care now. It was not like when I was labeled "fat" as a kid, my mindset has changed! Each time I had an interview, I told myself, "Please just label my ass," "Label it "cyberstalking," -one word," and "Let's get this moving forward because I was on a mission!"

I wanted justice..."**Moore Justice**" in fact, then I had received and **"Moore Justice"** than to be told I was crazy, and to be ignored. I knew I wasn't the only one experiencing cyberstalking. That added more fuel to my fire, more motivation to "get this show on the road." To label, define it and legislatively address it! That was the goal. I made sure it happened, and it did happen!

Promoting positive social change and working towards the common goal of eradicating abuse of any kind including stalking and cyberabuse, is my goal now!

Eradicating cyberstalking and abuse hasn't happened yet. It will take all of us collaborating to accomplish such a monumental movement. By uniting from all around the world, every age, gender, sexual orientation, and creed putting aside our differences, we can bring about positive social change. I believe this, or I would not waste my "time" fighting for it to be so!

I wrote this book, and I continue to speak, educate and inform, doing what I can to promote positive social change, because I will never get the time back that I lost in hell enduring it all. However, I feel that by saving others from losing precious time and grief, I am honoring my late grandmother and doing what I know I can to bring about reform to ensure no victim is left behind.

CHAPTER 4

What Do "Cyberpredators" Want?

On some level, in their worldview, cyberpredators believe that you have caused them harm. And they want you to pay. They often feel justified in doing so, even if the upset wasn't your choice, your responsibility, or your fault. They perceive you as the source of their pain, and therefore you must pay. Their "pain" could be the result of many things. A firing, a promotion they didn't get, a failed business deal, an eviction, a bad date, a break- up, a divorce, a custody battle, or a lost parking spot. But in their eyes, you somehow benefited from their pain or loss, and in return, you are now their target.
Why would someone want to do this to you?

They Want to Scare You!

Jane's Story

Jane was a successful realtor with business savvy and a contact list that wouldn't quit. Her work put her in the public eye, but she kept her home life sacred by making sure her home address and private phone number was not available to the public. One beautiful Saturday afternoon, her privacy was shattered, when among the usual junk, unsolicited magazines and bills she found an envelope from a client. The letter came addressed to Ms. Jane Bridge, Realtor.

"This is odd that it's coming here," she thought. She opened up the envelope, which had an Oklahoma postmark. She began to feel that strange fear, the "uh oh." She pulled a white piece of lined paper out of the envelope and read: "Jane Bridge you are going to get it — you bitch!"

Jane cried out, and she dropped the letter. Her husband came running, and they both stared at the paper together. Jane was beside herself. She had been a Realtor for 15 years, and there had been plenty of scuffs and scrapes along the way. All Realtors deal with upset clients at one point or another. But this was different. Someone had gone out of their way to find out where she lived and they were letting her know it.

Jane tried to think of who it could be, but it only made matters worse. She met so many people at work, and there had been the inevitable transactions that didn't go through, houses that sold for too little or weren't sold in time to meet conditional offers or people who lost their dream house to higher bidders. It could be anyone. At the same time, she never thought that something like this could happen. It was overwhelming.

From that point on, Jane carried pepper spray in her purse, always met clients at her office, and she never showed a house alone. She always looks over her shoulder and to this day has trouble opening an envelope that is not familiar to her. This one event changed Jane's life forever.

Sometimes a cyberstalker just wants to scare you. A cyberstalkers intention is to get at emotional reaction out of you to compensate for the upset they experienced and feel you are responsible.

Their goal is to put the fear in you and make you question your safety. In Jane's case, it didn't go further, but the incident put her on edge for a long time. It even made her question the career she loved. Someone sent a pretty strong message..."I know where you live."

Scare tactics can escalate, from threatening emails and text messages to using information gained online to harass you.

My cyberstalker used the information he knew about my shaky financial situation, (most of which he had caused of course), to send process servers and debt collectors after me. It is a frighteningly simple maneuver to pull on anyone who owes money, or even who is in the process of sorting out a divorce and might not even be responsible for certain bills --except that their name is still on the account.

These process servers are not well-dressed businessmen from the credit card company who come for tea. No, it's way more "Wild West." Process servers are sketchy third parties hired by the collection company or a law firm to get their client's money back. These are not nice people. Certainly not the kind of people you want banging on your door on a Saturday

It's a pretty simple thing to send processor servers to someone if it's perceived, rightly or wrongly, that that person owes money. All my cyberstalker had to do was call up the lawyer that was hired by the collection agency and say, "Alexis says she doesn't have the money, but I happen to know she does. She's living here at this address..." He'd once again tracked down my new place. "And by the way, she's got a gun."

The collection companies didn't stop to verify the information. They didn't look at the court records that stated I wasn't responsible for those bills or that, in fact, I honestly and truly had no money. Instead, they sent two scary dudes, who started kicking in my door at 9 am. They looked like they were straight out of a gangster movie, and their guns were real. They were there to get money. I was scared out of my mind. By the time the police arrived, the process servers had left. I filed the police report, and the misunderstanding was sorted out. My day was gone, I was left terrified of what tomorrow would bring. I'm sure my cyberstalker was very satisfied with himself that day!

They Want to Humiliate You and Destroy Your Reputation

Another way for a cyberstalker to "get you" is by humiliating you and damaging your reputation. This tactic resembles more closely to the "cyberbullying" school of tactics, though it can get even more intense than a nasty forum poster or high school bully with access to social media.

Brian's Story

Brian was a successful real estate investor and also the CEO of a property management company. He was a wealthy man who had many attorneys and advisors to protect his legal and financial interests. He never thought that a cyberstalker could hurt him. One of Brian's tenants thought differently. She became angry when Brian came for past due rent payments and proceeded to cyberstalk him for four years. She tracked his activities using common online locating techniques. She identified each of his private addresses and sent mail to each of his homes and business addresses. She sent mail as well as emails to his other tenants. She spread lies about him on online, on business rating sites. She posted lies about him on many real estate professional sites that his friends and colleagues used.

At first, Brian was unconcerned, but after time, he went to the police for help. No one took him seriously, and no one could help. For Brian, the results were devastating. He became depressed and overwhelmed. His marriage did not survive the cyberstalking. He was caught completely off guard and couldn't deal with the humiliation and despair that his cyberstalker caused. We were eventually able to stop Brian's cyberstalker, but from Brian's point of view, it was too late.

They Want to Damage You Financially

Cyberstalkers take great joy in hurting us financially. It makes for a great revenge tactic as our finances are the key to our economic, emotional, and physical well-being. Plus, our financial information is, quite conveniently situated for the cyberstalker, because it is deeply dependent on online information and technological systems, including the ever popular online business rating sites like Yelp, BBB, and Google+. Thus your finances are a prime target for a cyberstalker, particularly for cyberstalkers who may have invested in your economic collapse. It can be from someone you know, such as an abusive ex, seeking to maintain control or a competitor who is all too eager to see your business fail!

Methods for Cyberpredators to "Cash-In" - Without Taking a Dime!

There are many ways that the cyberstalker can get your banking information or mess with your credit rating. They can drain your bank account and make it impossible to get credit, and this can also lead to a secondary "benefit" of humiliating you since employers and landlords often look at this information when deciding whether to work with you. Bankruptcy is a familiar outcome of being cyberstalked. It's often one of the only ways you can wipe the slate clean and start over. That is what happened to me.

There are other subtle ways that a cyberstalker can put your finances in jeopardy. It is an ever growing problem that is the expanding along with consumer's use of online business rating sites such as Yelp, Google+, BBB and even the residential neighborhood social site that is growing ever so popular "Nextdoor." There will be more to come, as technology continues to grow, and this only adds more ammunition for the ways a cyberstalker will continue to garner financial control over victims.

One client, let's call her Becca, had a vengeful ex who took his upset out on not only her but the people closest to her. He managed to shut down Becca's brother and sister-in-law's business website for a couple of days and turned their once successful web-based small business into a failing entity that was nearing bankruptcy.

Their web store was their only source of income, and he hit it at a peak ordering time. Not only did they lose the business during the time the website was down, but they also lost customer confidence... how often do you go back to a site that wasn't working the last time you were there?

Not to mention the fact the online business ratings for the web business were plummeting – the business that once had a pristine 5-star rating was now experiencing the cyber-plummet. The customers were rating the business with 1 star online, and posts began to pile up stating, "How slow and miserable..." and "No one should ever do business with them." These negative online reviews coupled with the attacks that the cyberstalker had already begun posting online, long before the web crash, made it nearly impossible for the business to pull out of the cyberstalkers attack!

Becca's brother and sister-in-law calculated that in total they lost about $30,000 worth of business as a result of real-time sales loss. Not to mention the permanent trail of bad reviews online, that were piling up one after the other on the social business rating sites. These negative online reviews have the more devastating effect as they are far too often long lasting, and the business reputation and goodwill are something very hard to replace. Once it is gone, it is gone forever in most instances. Some ultimately end up having to change their business names or do "grand openings" in an attempt to overcome these kinds of attacks but these are futile in most instances, and the permanent loss is often sadly inevitable.

Why Cyberabuse targeting Financial Loss will continue

Sadly, most don't understand how easy it is for a vicious cyberpredator to bankrupt a person anonymously; in particular, a small business owner who is attempting to live the "American Dream." Entrepreneurs are the ones whom I have the greatest respect. They get out of bed every morning and drive their own business and have such a great responsibility on their shoulders. It is much easier to be an employee and to clock in and to clock out. Sadly, because of the cyberabuse taking place today, I see many small business owners and amazing people lose their luster...their "entrepreneurial spirit" because of the vicious online world of today.

The negative online business ratings coupled with the website crash made it nearly impossible for this couple to regain their fiscal position that was once before very comfortable.

Worse yet, trying to explain that a cyberstalker had targeted them, certainly was not conducive to business. The owners were spending valuable time replying to negative online reviews and explaining to customers that should have been spent engaging in their business activities – earning a living.

Most consumers have no empathy or sympathy, and truly just don't care until and unless of course it happens to them and cyberpredators are relying on this fact. This mindset has to change. It is vital, as we get further engulfed into a more and more "cyber society." What societal norm needs, is to include the fact that cyberabuse is real, and we must learn as a society not to support cyberpredators by our actions.

It is so critical for society at large to understand the methods used by cyberstalkers so that there can be social change. If this does not happen, the "American Dream" is going to be very short-lived for many and may even become non-existent.

All of us play a role. We simply must help do what we can to remain aware and open-minded. Online reviews and what gets published on the web are not the gospel. It is not always the truth. Anyone, at any time, can publish online reviews for example and do so anonymously even.

The financial loss for victims of cyberabuse that are business owners and entrepreneurs is a growing problem and will far too often be a dire situation because the economic attacks perpetrated by cyberstalkers often never goes away.

The business owner has to wait until there is an online "upswing" and work very hard to restore their online reputation. That can take years as well as literally thousands of hours and worse yet, cost vast amounts of money if hiring so-called "online reputation management services." Cyberpredators know this, they are relying on the ignorance of society and the ever growing use of these rating sites to be the "norm" so that they can continue to attack and do so without any recourse.

Victims engaging with lawyers can be futile as well. I know from experience working with cyberabuse victims who are business owners and entrepreneurs. They found it very difficult to find an attorney willing to take their case, much less any reward if they did, because of the 1st amendment protections and the lax regulations governing the "social sites."

There must be added protections for victims. There must be an evolution in our legislature and in our societal mindset that includes legislating with the fact in mind that cyberabuse is real and that victims...millions of them, in fact, deserve protection!

Otherwise, the devastating isolation of victims will continue as more and more innocent people find themselves bankrupt, starting over, and disillusioned.

CHAPTER 5

They Want to Isolate You

This example leads us to another way that a cyberstalker can get to you, which is to isolate you from your family and community. Becca's brother and sister-in-law were none too happy to be swept into what they considered her problems, particularly when it started to impact their life and business. The relationship soured, and there were two fewer people Becca could count on for help, comfort, and support. Even after the cyberstalking finally ceased, that relationship still hasn't healed.

A nasty cyberstalker will attack the people in their target's life, because the more they make other people miserable, the more they isolate their intended target. When people are mad at you for the inconvenience, upset, loss, or fear they are experiencing, it can damage relationships permanently. It doesn't seem fair, but when people experience threatening experiences over a long period, fair doesn't enter into it. Eventually, they want you and your problems to go away and for their lives to go back to normal.

It also means that when you tell other people that your cyberstalker has targeted people in your life, they become reluctant to get involved with you either in friendship or support. I can't tell you how many lawyers quit on me because they couldn't deal with my situation. It was very lonely, and it was the source of my greatest depression.

My grandmother who was supportive of me experienced attacks online and offline. It made it very difficult for me not to feel guilty, and not to feel that if I were not part of her life, she would not be experiencing the abuse. What made it worse yet was the response I received from those around me, including complete strangers!

My grandmother was followed by private investigators hired by my ex and reported these instances to the police. She was picking up my mail and helping me because I was in hiding, hoping that if I stayed below the radar for a week or two, I would be able to outlast him and get my life back. That is not what happened, and matters became extremely worse.

My grandmother was in hospice care and had nurses coming in and out all hours of the day and night. It wasn't long before she was housebound and not able to drive, but she remained outspoken and my strongest ally.

It wasn't until the phone in her home began to ring off the hook all hours of the day and night that I began to sink deep into a depression. The phone was not ringing because of concerned relatives checking in or friends. Instead, it was bill collectors. My cyberstalker had given them her telephone number too, saying it was my contact number and that I was a day sleeper. They were calling day and night making it nearly impossible for us to keep the phone on the hook. My grandmother took this in stride saying, "Someday Alexis, you will be a lawyer and will sue these bastards! She was right about that!

Nevertheless, on one of my visits, my grandmother was fast asleep, as I sat on the couch quietly reading and half dosing until my grandmother awakened so that I could visit with her.

I will never forget the nurses as they circled me. They felt like piranhas. One of them said, "Alexis, you need to go away and leave your grandmother alone. You are causing her too much stress, and it is your fault!" I didn't know what to say. I was startled, and of course didn't want to hurt my grandmother in any way. I loved her and would never want to hurt her. As I was gathering my purse and coat to leave, I heard this thud and stomping around. Then, I heard my grandmother calling my name saying, "Alexis don't you dare leave." She had gotten out of bed on her own and came, literally flying into the living area where I was standing, and told the nurses, "My granddaughter is not leaving! If anyone is leaving and not welcome, it is all of you!"

I had to laugh a little, at that moment I had forgotten how sick she was. I saw only the brave woman who had been encouraging me all of these months, and even in her last months she never gave up on me or said what a burden it was. Even though I know what a burden it was, I wish I could erase the entire experience, and she never had to have endured this horrible situation. But the remarkable part of this experience is that this is what the cyberstalker wanted! My abuser was hoping to isolate me and get me to the lowest place a human being can be, where you feel that you have no hope and no way to ever overcome.

I didn't leave. Instead, I put down my purse and asked the "piranhas" to sit down. LOL...they were not piranhas. In fact, they were very nice women that were trying to help, even though their actions nearly destroyed me. The room was silent, the only thing I remember was the sound of the oxygen tank as it puffed the air into my grandmother through the nasal cannula. My thoughts quickly gathered, and my grandmother sat beside me, holding my hand. It was then that the advocate in me was born.

I explained I was a domestic violence victim, and that I was a "victim of stalking," and that the predator was using "electronic means to stalk me as well."

I explained what had happened to me, looking them right in the eyes, with my face literally on fire from anger. But there was also this fierce passion that now was burning inside me.

My words were strong and fierce. I hammered in the fact that, I had no control over the abuser's actions, and if I had had the control I would have stopped him long ago! But alas, this is where I was at this moment in time. I told them that law enforcement would not take any action, and explained that the district attorney had said that I have no criminal case that they can prosecute. I also told them about my attorneys quitting on me.

I continued explaining to the women it was not my intent to harm my grandmother in any way, but if I were to go away and "be gone" as they suggested, I would lose what precious time with her I had left. I explained that that was something I wouldn't and couldn't do and that if I did my predator would win, even more than he already had.

"So now, I hope you understand a little bit more, and that you will take pause the next time you encounter a situation that perhaps doesn't seem right and see it from another point of view," I said as I finished speaking.

The ladies were now still. Their faces, I remember like yesterday, went from full of color to white as a ghost! They probably thought they had seen a ghost and may have been scared as hell as well! I suspect I would have been as well if someone told me this scary story.

The ladies said they were glad I had my grandmother and my grandmother, of course, said she was "very lucky to have me as her granddaughter." They said nothing more after this occasion.

I was lucky in this instance. I fought off the isolation that victim's experience. Sadly most victims don't have the advocate within. It is a skill that is learned and comes from having the support of another human being even if it comes from just one person.

I am far too often that one person and I want help to change that. Knowing that the attempt to isolate me was now, over and that I was not alone was helpful, but that didn't stop my concerns about how the stalker and cyberstalker were keeping tabs on me.

CHAPTER 6

They Want to Keep Tabs on You

There are enough stalker stories out there to make you want to stay home with the curtains drawn and never come out. What often doesn't get noticed or reported in a story is how traditional stalkers use cyberstalking methods to track the object of their obsession.

An example is that of Stefani, a woman who did everything right in her efforts to stay ahead of her stalker. She dated a man for three years, and after their relationship had ended, she cut off all contact. He tried through various ways to get in touch with her. When she didn't respond, he began to stalk her, her new boyfriend, and her family. Stefani was the true target, however, and even with a restraining order and constant reports to the police, it was clear things were getting worse and law enforcement couldn't or wouldn't take action.

Stefani moved from New Mexico to California and tried to protect herself and the location of her new location. She got a private mail box (Mail Drop / UPS Store) and a new cell phone. She reported her problem immediately to the local authorities and even met with her neighbors to show them her stalker's photo and urge them to call police if they saw him. All of her efforts did not work. With the help of a private investigator, who used online tracking methods, Stefani's cyberstalker was able to to find her again and murder her just two weeks before her case against him went to trial.

Stefani was not my client. But her story is one that I am determined never to have repeated. It is the foundation behind why I say it is so important not to take time for granted, and also why it's so important to take incidents of stalking and cyberstalking seriously.

Many times, stalking homicides involves a victim doing everything right. They use the existing tools available like restraining orders and take the advice of law enforcement, but this is sadly often not enough. That is why I speak out and continue to share what I know from helping myself and others.

Technology, antiquated legislation and law enforcement techniques give cyberpredators and stalkers the upper hand.
For a victim to survive in today's environment, the victims have to make their safety and security another "full-time job." What I mean by this is that in addition to the existing family and work obligations, along with the usual priorities of life, victims of cyberabuse and stalking now have to make space in their lives to create time for diligently protecting themselves. Accomplishing this is no easy chore, it is hour by hour, day by day obligation and there are no days off or paid leave. **It is full-time, all the time.**

It is the reason why so many victims feel depressed and suffer from PTSD. The human flight or fight response is not meant to be on 24/7. Just ask any Veteran who has returned home from the battlefield. The experience of being "on" all the time takes its toll on a person. It is truly exhausting.

I know because I lived it. I was "on" and still am 24/7. Rather making this a burden, like full-time 2nd or 3rd jobs would be, I make it a fact of life that I understand and live. It took me time to learn how to evolve and adjust as a human being and make this being "on" a normal and regular part of life.

I want to share what I know because learning how to be "on" and not zap every ounce of energy I had for other things, took time and effort to learn. It did not come easy.

Defending and overcoming cyberabuse and stalking is no easy task. Knowing more of the "cyberpredators tricks of the trade," and what I know has worked to help victims overcome and defend cyberabuse and stalking is what I am hoping will help. It is my mission that you will get more time to live life without having to start over again, or worse yet, lose your life because time and life is far too precious.

These cyberstalking tricks of the trade are only some of the methods that the predators use. There are going to be millions more, and one is foolish to think that there won't be something new but overall the basics "the cyberattack core methods" will always be the same.

The good news, the predator will use the existing technology that is intended for "one purpose" for "another." It truly is this simple. Keeping that in mind and always understanding that the type of technology will change but not the motives one has a fighting chance to defend and overcome and quite easily in fact.

CHAPTER 7

Cyberstalking Tricks of the Trade

We freely post personal information on social and business networking sites and share financial information with online vendorsandfinancialinstitutions.Themomentthatourinformation is online, we forever lose control of it and open ourselves up to cyberattacks. Further, there are very few consumer protections in place to regulate the companies called data brokers, and the individuals that request and transmit our information. Look to any news headline about a data breach where millions of consumer's information are hacked or stolen due to predators. It's not hard to see we are fighting an uphill and often sadly a losing battle.

We must realize that the information that we share online, including on "private" social and business networking sites, creates a wealth of information that cyberstalkers can later harvest.
The damage that cyberstalkers do ranges from just plain creepy and scary to the devastating. The most common cyberstalking techniques used today include:

Email Attacks and Email Bombs

Cyberstalkers love email just as much as the rest of us. Unfortunately, while we use email to connect with others and conduct business, they use email to harass us, as well as the people in our lives. Harassment may come in the form of threatening emails directly from your cyberstalker. Often, however, these email attacks are directed specifically to the families, friends, and co-workers. These emails often include threatening, hateful, or obscene language or photos that are meant to embarrass or humiliate you. These email attacks often occur on a regular basis so that you have a difficult time finding out who is sending them so that you can't undo the damage to your reputation.

Online Impersonation and Email Forgery

Few online sites require that you verify who you are when you sign up for a new account. You can enter any name and address that you want. These lax registration procedures also make it very easy for a cyberstalker to impersonate you. By creating a new account and user profile, using your name and even your photo if they have one, a cyberstalker can impersonate you on message boards, forums, and networking sites. They may leave offensive or inflammatory comments on your behalf. The negative reactions that occur will, of course, be pointing to you, not the cyberstalker.

Online impersonation is another very dangerous form of cyberabuse and often involves the use of what is labeled as sextortion a form of exploitation/blackmail in which sexual information or images are used to extort sexual favors from the victim. Social media and text messages are often the source of the sexual material and the threatened means of sharing it with others.

Non-consensual Pornography is the sexually explicit portrayal of one or more people that is distributed, without their consent via any medium.

The sexual assault epidemic labeled "stealthing;" where the man without the consent of the other partner removes the condom during intercourse and then boasts about it online keeping "score" of their sick triumphs with others online.

Cyberstalkers often post personal stories or "confessions" when pretending to be their victim. Often, these confessions are of a sexual nature and posted with the intent of damaging reputations. More than being humiliating, this technique can also be physically dangerous. Jilted boyfriends and spouses have even been known to solicit rapes and physical attacks on their victims.

Online Misinformation and Defamation

We all love online social networking; Facebook, Twitter, LinkedIn, Snapchat, Instagram (and every other social platform that will come to exist "someday"). They allow us to connect with people, build our businesses, and expand our circles of influence around the world!
I can't say social media hasn't helped me. The sites have helped me to expand education about cyberstalking and stalking, promote legislative and advocacy efforts and allow for victims to find me to get help, but the sinister side of social media is that cyberstalkers and cyberpredators also love online networking, because it gives them a fantastic weapon to harm you. These networking sites are a key resource tool that cyberstalkers will use to learn about you and your life. For example, while it may be fun to have Facebook remind people that it is our birthday, it is quite dangerous to list your birthday. Our birthday often used as a security password by credit card and financial institutions.

Networking sites also give cyberstalkers access to an important contact list when they want to damage your reputation. By knowing which online social communities and social groups are most important to you, cyberstalkers also know how to best damage your reputation.

One of my clients experienced cyberstalking through his Facebook account. Since Bill's stalker had access to Bill's Facebook account, he had easy access to all of his friends. It was simple to circulate damaging rumors about Bill. Bill's stalker sent a Facebook message to everyone on Bill's friends list telling them that Bill had stolen money and warning everyone to watch out. Since Bill also had invited colleagues and co-workers to join his circle of friends, these attacks ruined his credibility until we could get the problem unraveled.

Hacking and Computer Control

Some cyberstalkers take things a step further and can gain control of their victim's online accounts or electronic devices altogether. When they gain access to your email and online account passwords, a cyberstalker would have the ability to check your email every day, the access to steal personal and financial data, email and phone contact lists, social networking site contacts, photos, etc.

When then gain access to your electronic devices they can remotely access your audio and camera and even listen in to your phone calls and conversations.

In my case, my ex was able to gain control of my computer and my email accounts using a spyware virus he sent electronically disguised as a Hallmark e-card.

About Keylogging

Key-logging, or keystroke logging, can be done in many different ways, and it is usually easy to detect if you are a fast typist - it will often make a computer run more slowly. If you pay attention, a lag time occurs. While you're typing, a delay or pause may occur before the letters appear on the screen that is the usual giveaway. But this is not the only way, and key logging virus is becoming more and more sophisticated.

Sometimes it's installed directly into the computer hardware- the "direct human to computer contact."
Keylogging also can be done by software-based programs. The software may be downloaded along with another program or by opening an attachment that has a virus. The program can run silently behind the scenes, either under the operating system or as part of it, making it difficult to detect. If it's a virus, most anti- spyware programs will detect it. It is also a good idea to get a computer pro to check out the machine if there's any suspicion of keylogging.

Keylogging programs collect each keystroke and relay it to another party via email, an FTP, or directly to another computer. Keylogging bypasses the security of https sites because it does not affect those sites in any way, it only records the information that's typed in, meaning it easily gains access to all passwords and login information.

The methods and abilities of a cyberstalker will continue to expand as rapidly as technology continues to advance.

My Personal experience with keylogging

My cyberstalker could log into my computer at any time to check on my contact lists, read my emails and had access to everything I was doing online.

I only became aware of the fact he had this "unlimited virtual access" when it was brought forth to my attorney's attention.
Because of the fact, the predator was giving opposing counsel copies of the emails between my lawyer and I it caught my attention, and I was able to do something about it.

My attorney at the time called me and was frantic. He said I needed to get right into his office, as he had something very important to show me. When I arrived, he showed me copies of the emails that were from me to my lawyer and said: "I have no fucking idea how this is possible, but holy shit I understand and believe you now Alexis, you are being- cyberstalked."

My solution: I armed myself with this information to give him a false trail to follow. Send emails, do research online and conduct my activities knowing that he was watching and reading. I sent emails to friends and family indicating I was moving, changing attorneys and had established a new intimate relationship. I discussed travel plans and new job opportunities that didn't exist. I completed online rental applications for rentals I would never live in. These methods bought me precious time offline that I desperately needed to get my life back.

I reported the activity to law enforcement, and they took no action. I wasn't surprised and didn't even think twice about it. I didn't expect any help.

I worked with the knowledge that I did have and used it to my advantage to give myself more time to do something else.

Email and Caller ID Spoofing

If your phone's Caller ID tells you that the Bank of America is calling, of course, it must be the Bank of America calling, right? Not true at all. Email and Caller ID spoofing allow us all to change the display name that displays on our emails, texts, and phone calls. Cyberstalkers know that people are trusting and they abuse this trust to obtain information about us.

I started to help educate the public years ago by saying "Trust Caller ID - Become a Victim." The folly of trusting Caller ID will remain true because, even with legislative efforts to stop it, such as, "The Truth in Caller ID Act," or any other law on the books making it illegal, the use of this tech and other sinister tech apps is profitable. Therefore, just when regulators shut down one

Spoof or similar tech another will pop up and in a jurisdiction that the US Laws won't reach.

Therefore, awareness is key. Being vigilant is key.

Geotagging, GPS monitoring "check-ins."

(Whatever it may be labeled) Today's online and mobile applications let us tell our friends where we are at all times. So if they happen to be in the same area of town, we could meet them for drinks. Or they can track which restaurants and bars we think are the best. And they'll know when we're home. But imagine that a cyberstalker or stalker had all of that information about you. He would know where you were at all times, when you were at home (or not), and with whom you had been associating. Aside from the plain creepiness of someone tracking our every move, it is very dangerous when that person wants to harm you.

Be Prepared and Defend Yourself

When faced with a cyberstalker, most people tend to curl up and want to die. Your fear is what these predators feed on! Your fear of what he or she could do next. Your fear of not knowing who is doing this to you. Your fear of being hurt or outcast in ways you can't imagine, and your fear of losing what you've got or being humiliated.

Cyberstalkers are cowards who love the power they get from your fear. That's why they keep coming back for more. But there are ways to defend yourself and your family. I am not an extremist who recommends that we all live off the grid and never again log onto a social networking site. Instead, I recommend taking charge of your online information and identity. Hiding in plain sight is my approach, and I encourage this because it works!

How to use this book going forward

In the next chapters, you will learn to develop what I call Solutions. Solutions that are designed to help you defend and overcome cyberabuse and stalking.

Compiled below are anecdotes of real life victims. Their stories describe what they have gone through, and how they resolved their situations. Cyberpredators and stalkers are creative they use what they have available to them. We, in response, must then be creative ourselves and use the powerful tools that we have!

By compiling these anecdotes and the Self-Defense Strategies, I am saving you time from having to do it yourself! No need to reinvent the wheel here.

Take from this what you need and discard what you don't. There is no "one size fits all approach" to anything in life, and that is particularly true when it comes to applying solutions to defending and overcoming cyberabuse and stalking.

What you have herein is what I know worked for me and has worked for others. It is a starting point, and from there you can add your "own creative touches" to it and make it work for you.
Saving time is the goal. Time is everything.

CHAPTER 8

Anecdotes and Solution Strategies

Sara's Story – Spoof Technology

Sara's phone startled her. She rolled out of bed and rushed to her purse. The caller ID showed it was her best friend, Aileen. Something terrible must have happened for Aileen to call at this time of night. No one calls much these days unless it's important, especially not when a text will do. Her fingers were trembling as Sara returned the phone call.

A groggy voice answered. After Sara had demanded to know what was wrong, Aileen responded with aggravation, "Why did wake me up in the middle of the night?" "But you called me!" Sara asserted. Aileen, who had been in a deep sleep, was adamant that she hadn't made any calls.

"You had a dream, Sara," she said. "Go back to sleep. And don't call me in the middle of the night again unless it's an emergency." Stephanie stared at her phone. It showed Aileen's number as an incoming call at 3:43 in the morning. She hadn't been dreaming.

The next morning Sara arrived at school Aileen was amusing a small group of classmates with the tale of Sara's late night call. She pulled out her phone and showed them the number. They all shrugged it off as being nothing.

Later that day Sara's phone rang. With a glimpse at the number, she quickly silenced it off. Her sister knew she wasn't allowed to take personal calls at work. Why was she calling in the middle of the school day? It must be an emergency. She put her phone into her pocket and rushed into the hall to return the call. As Aileen had the night before, Sara's sister claimed she hadn't called.

Still shaken, Sara stepped out into the hall and almost ran into Ian, one of the tech guys in the school's administration office. He said she looked shaken and asked if anything was wrong. Sara revealed the two calls, and Ian expressed his understanding. Being kind, he made a jest about how wires get crossed and went down the hall.

The strange calls continued. Friends and classmates called and texted, yet when Sara responded, they acted mystified and said they hadn't called or texted. The toughest ones were the calls in the middle of the night. She couldn't overlook them because they might be emergencies. After returning a few of the late-night calls and waking her friends and classmates from sleep, Sara stopped phoning back. She'd toss and turn the rest of the night, but wait until morning to respond back. Each time she did, she got the same reply. None of them had called or texted her.

She was starting to wonder if she was going nuts. And others wondered the same thing. Only a few people at school listened to her stories. Most people just rolled their eyes and walked off. Her friend Ben even asked if Sara was doing this to get attention. After that, Sara clammed up.

Then Sara began getting calls in the middle of the night from the guardhouse of her gated apartment community. Guards checked on single women who requested it, or they responded to alarm calls. Although she hadn't asked to be checked on, she answered just in case they were issuing a security warning.

Nobody was on the line when she picked up the phone.
The other calls had been more infuriating or embarrassing, but these scared her. Again, when she mentioned the calls to friends at class, most snubbed her or told her to get a new phone. Only Aileen and Ian still listened and sent caring tweets or texts.

The anxiety and late-night calls were taking a toll on Sara. Her grades were slipping, and she had trouble staying focused during the day. She was scared to answer the phone, and she'd lost the trust of her friends and family who didn't believe her. Even her sister thought she was crazy.

Then she experienced a terrifying night. Stephanie woke to the sound of her cell phone ringing and the caller ID showed it was Aileen calling. She answered, and on the other end a deep, horror-movie voice said, "I know where you live, bitch." The message ended with loud noise and whistling that pierced Sara's ear. She stayed awake all night, paralyzed with fear.

Sara's Solutions

Frantic and scared, Sara contacted **Survivors in Action** for help. She was relieved to learn that she wasn't going crazy. What she'd been experiencing were spoof calls and texts. Using a simple spoof card, all the perpetrator had to know was Stephanie's phone number and those of her family and friends. The card allows cyberpredators, "spoofers" to change their phone number to any number they desire. It's easy for the spoofer to call or send text messages to someone else, for example, the phone company, the gate guard, a friend, a neighbor, or relative. If they know the phone number, they can make calls using that number.

As with every cyberabuse case, I encouraged Sara to report it to law enforcement. Sara's small-town police department was not aware of spoofing technology. I contacted them and provided documentation that such technology existed to help them realize Sara was telling the truth.

Understanding what was happening was a great relief to Sara. She knew now she wasn't going crazy as her classmates and family suggested. With the proof I provided, Sara convinced her family, friends, and classmates that what had happened to her was real and could happen to them too. In this way, she began to gain back her confidence.

"Moore" Solutions to Defend Yourself

In addition to reporting the incident to the police, Sara changed her phone number. With the help of her sister, Sara bought a new phone and her sister added her on her wireless account. Sara only gave the number out to family and a few trusted friends to start.

In the past, she'd shared her number with all of her classmates and on social media. Now she kept her phone number as private as she could. She had no idea who the cyberspoofer was, so she took no chances of the predator getting her information again.

Self-Help Action Steps to Take

- Stay in control and don't panic, because that will give the cyberabuser gratification.
- If you suspect spoofing, take screen shots and start documenting right away.
- Keep an Events Timeline. Record all dates, times, and calls and save the screen shots to a file separate from your phone.

•   Get the public safety paper trail started! Contact law enforcement and report the incidents; having a record can help if the incidents escalate. If law enforcement doesn't take a report in person, report the activity online. Even if you have to use identity theft as the label of your spoofing experiences report it – get the public safety paper trail going. Print the online report before you send it for your records.

•   When reporting incidents by phone or in person, stay calm, matter-of-fact, and maintain your composure. Remaining calm is key because law enforcement is much less likely to take your case seriously if you don't. They do not understand the stress you are under; they are not living your life, so remaining as calm as you can is a big part of success in reporting a cyberabuse or stalking case.

•   Ask a friend, classmate, family member, attorney or coworker to accompany you to the police station. It may help you to feel more comfortable and is possible that your situation will be considered more seriously.

•   Consult with a lawyer, cybercrime experts, a risk management consultant (like myself), or a private investigator as needed.

•   Continue to report the incidents and keep track of them in an Events Timeline that you maintain.

•   Don't talk about the incidents in public or with others using social media because the cyberpredator may be monitoring you and listening to your reactions. They want you to react!

•   If you discover the cyberpredator don't confront them, this could be dangerous.

Identification of the Cyberpredator

When Sara realized that law enforcement would not be investigating her cyberabuse case, we decided to see if together we could figure out who the predator was.

Identifying the predator helps to defend against further instances of cyberabuse and if they escalate giving a name to the police is a good way to get the investigation going. Cyberabuse cases are difficult to investigate, to begin with, and when victims report to law enforcement and have absolutely no idea who it could be, that makes getting support even less likely.

In Sara's case, although it could have been a stranger, after examining the incidents carefully I believed it was most likely someone she knew. I based my opinion on the fact that the cyberpredator was using friends and family phone numbers.

A stranger using this tech is trying to commit fraud or identity theft. Often they will use the technology to mimic a "bank" or "IRS employee," in attempts to garner the personal identifiers of the victim so that they can perpetrate identity theft or fraud for financial gain, etc. against a potential suspect.

As Sara grew more and more anxious and was being called crazy by her classmates, friends, and family, it was a payday for "Mr. IT Guy", Ian. Sara may not have paid attention to him on or offline before, but she certainly did now...and at 2 a.m.

The cyberpredator had her undivided attention, and without her even knowing it was controlling a big part of her life.
Even better, he was following Sara on social media, and he was reading her posts where she was expressing her disgust with having one sleepless night after the other, and not being able to catch up on homework assignments. He was getting the "cyberpredator high" of her telling classmates about the strange calls and was all too happy with himself, knowing he was causing chaos in her life!

All the while, he was sending her supportive emails and texts, and posting on social media his support of her, wishing her well, Sara responded, which was fulfilling his need for attention in a bunch of different ways.

Sara ended up finishing school, and together we reported our suspicions to the school officials regarding "Mr. IT Guy." The school officials couldn't do anything and Sara hired a private investigator and tried to find enough evidence for a lawyer to take her case and sue the school and "Mr. IT Guy," but we couldn't find any attorneys willing to take her case on contingency and the statute of limitations had run out.

Sara and I stay connected, she graduated and is teaching 7th grade and shares her story to help educate others.

When I provide direct support to victims taking "the time" I hold so precious, I choose cases where I feel the victim will take charge and fight back right along beside me.

There are too many victims in need reaching out for help, that I find it impossible to serve them all. My work needs to be accomplished wisely, quickly and efficiently. I have the painstaking task of triaging cases and choosing to work with victims that I can help in the shortest amount of time possible. It requires their 100% dedication and active participation.

In this case, the predator was obviously seeking a "reaction." The calls and texts in the middle of the night that disrupted her sleep habits and ability to concentrate on her studies made it obvious to me that the cyberpredator was more than likely someone that she knew. It was a matter of figuring out who had the motive and the contact with Sara.

"The Events Time Line" is the most powerful weapon a victim has to be able to defend and overcome against cyberpredators and stalkers more quickly. It is a precious time saver.

In Sara's case, the goal was for her time to be spent focused on her studies and with her family and friends, not being anxious and nervous and awake at night.

Keeping a journal called, "The Events Time Line" allows a 3rd party, such as law enforcement, attorneys and advocates like me, a way to create an escape route and back to life plan that otherwise one would not have. **KEEP THE JOURNAL** and update it this needs to be the top priority!

The cyberpredators, in this case, a "spoofer," is most likely someone who'd get an adrenaline rush what I call "the cyberpredator high," by making Sara upset. A scorned ex, jealous classmate or coworker is often the culprit, but not in Sara's case.

It turned out that the only people who'd showed any real interest in Sara's unending "cybersaga," was Aileen and Ian, the IT guy from her school.

Before the spoof calls, she had never spoken to him unless she needed tech help and that was not very often. However, he had taken an interest in Sara and seemed to be around a lot. He was following her on social media and was suddenly extremely caring and overly interested. Because he'd sent her repeated supportive texts and began following her on social media "Mr. IT" was on my radar as a possible suspect.

CHAPTER 9

Karin's Story

Beware of What You Share

Karin and Jess had been friends for years. They grew up together, living right across the street from one another. Like most BFF's, they shared everything including their passwords. They also shared the most intimate details of their lives with one another, just as most friends do.

Then Jess began hanging around with the more popular kids, and the bullying and practical jokes began, all at Karin's expense. Jess fit in with the "in-crowd," whereas Karin just didn't. She tried to do so on many occasions, which only made matters worse. She was not as fit as the other girls and wasn't into hair and makeup, so her attempts to be "that" person was futile at best. In most cases, it backfired even. She preferred the quieter side of life. Reading and writing were her passion, and she kept a journal.   Karin was an excellent writer. In fact, she had been number one in the student writing competition that year and was aspiring to be an author someday. She was working hard to be accepted into a prestigious college so that she could get her Masters in Literature.

Jess knew this and was a bit jealous of Karin. Writing came so easily for Karin, while Jess struggled to get through English class and she nearly flunked the class several times!

One day Karin, who was shy and ashamed of her curvy shape was changing in gym class. Sari, one of the popular girls, snapped a picture and circulated it with #BiggestLoser on it!

A few days later, Sari had someone trip Karin in the hallway, causing her to fall and rip her pants up the backside. This time, Sari tweeted a video of the fall and Karin on the hall floor, holding her pants on by their seams. There was "GIF" created which was deeply humiliating for Karin.

Next, tweets and posts appeared on Karin's social media pages, revealing many thoughts and fantasies she'd written in her journal over the years. They were intimate details about her dates and other private information. Karin felt mortified beyond belief.
Karin's words were very powerful. She was an excellent writer, and the intimate thoughts and details were explicit, and to her chagrin, she spared no detail!

Even worse, was the posts to social media of "Karin's fantasies." These posts looked as if they'd come from Karin herself. She pretended to be sick to avoid going to school and was very depressed.

To make matters worse, over the weekend her phone "lit up" as she received hundreds of texts and social messages from many guys from school inviting her to "hang out and fulfill their fantasies."

She was horrified to learn that messages had been sent from her account, saying that "if they asked her out, she'd fulfill their fantasies," and after reading all of her "fantasies" online, they had suggestions for what they'd like her to do with them!

Karin knew of only one person who would be able to do this. Jess. Jess knew all of her passwords. Karin wanted to talk to Jess in person and let her know how much her actions had hurt her. She believed Jess still had the caring heart she'd had when they were BFFs.

She showed up at Jess's house unannounced. At first, Jess denied that she had anything to do with it. As they talked, Jess admitted that Sari had pressured her to reveal the passwords and secrets. Jess, who desperately wanted to be accepted, had given Sari everything she'd asked. As long as Jess was participating, she was the center of attention in the popular crowd; it was something she'd always dreamed of for herself.

She regretted leaking Karin's secrets but acknowledged that given a chance to be admired by Sari's group, she'd probably betray a friend again. For her, attention was more important than any moral code.

Karin learned a painful lesson about sharing with anyone, even a BFF, her passwords. She still had to face everyone at school. She knew her father wouldn't allow her to stay home the following week, so her only choices were to skip school or endure the humiliation of walking down the halls.

Karin's Solution

That weekend Karin's aunt probed to find out why her niece was reluctant to attend classes.

Her sister, Karin's mother, had died years before of ovarian cancer. She had taken on the mother role with Karin. She knew Karin was depressed and acting "off" and she didn't know why.

When she discovered what was going on, she reached out to Survivors in Action. Karin followed the Self-Help Action Steps

I suggested. First, she changed her passwords and reporting the posts.

Preventing new posts and deleting the messages were priorities. Because the posts were on Karin's account, it was easy for her to delete them quickly. What she couldn't do so easily was erase their impact and the damage to her reputation. Only time would do that.

She ended up writing a generic message saying: "My accounts were hacked from 1-24 to 1-31, so if you saw or received any messages from me during those dates, they were fake."

She posted it on all of her social media accounts and texted everyone in her contacts. Those that responded would be part of her life, those that didn't; she didn't need them anymore. That was very important. She had learned the value of trust and friendship and didn't want to repeat the same mistakes she had with Jess.

SIA volunteers helped her get the locker photos and videos removed from the net.

Karin didn't report the incidents. She elected to move forward. She knew who the cyber predators were, and she knew why they did what they did. She had what she felt was closure, and could move forward with her life now.

Her decision was to move on and never to forget the life lesson: passwords are private and never shared. Not with anyone. She also has placed a higher value on trust and loyalty, a life lesson that she now agrees was better to learn sooner than later.

Self-Help Action Steps to Take

- Make sure the message you send out about the cyberabuse is unemotional, to prevent the predator from getting satisfaction.

- Speak out! Report the incidents. You can do this anonymously.

CHAPTER 10

Morgan's Story

Exuberant and excited after winning their championship game, the collegiate football team headed to the bar after the game. They chose a table in the back. Morgan was clinging close to Kim, and when she pulled out a chair, he grabbed the seat next to her. But before she sat down, Cullen stood up and waved her over from the other side of the table, and Kim rushed around to join him.

Morgan slumped down in his seat. Of course, she'd prefer Cullen's company; he'd scored the winning goal.

He tried to console himself that he had a better view of Kim this way, but it didn't ease the jealousy eating away at his core. Morgan sat the bench most of the time. Injured during the off- season, it was difficult for him to watch all the "man worship" heaped on Cullen and Amar, who'd scored the winning touchdowns. He sat staring down into his cold beer and often glanced at his phone, as everyone around him chattered excitedly. They poured it on thick as they went over in vivid details of the best plays, and bad ass defensive moves – none of which were his.

"Cullen you were so freaking amazing," Kim declared, leaning over to kiss Cullen's cheek.

Unlucky in Love

Morgan winced. He'd had his eye on Kim for some time now, but he still hadn't worked up the courage to ask her out. The more she drank, the more boisterous Kim became, and the more affectionate. She was spreading her love, sharing kisses with the teammates around her and getting pretty drunk.

And the more Morgan drank, the more peeved he got. He added whiskey now, with his beer back. It sickened him that Cullen, a married man, slung his arm around Kim's shoulders and pulled her so close she was practically sitting in his lap – they needed a room, it was getting that bad!

Ariela, the American transplant who still insisted on calling the game soccer, tried to include Morgan in the conversation, but he could tell she was only doing it to be nice. After getting a few grumpy, one-word answers from him, she shrugged and turned to chat with the player on her right.

Morgan had a strict religious upbringing, and the more he drank, the louder his minister father's voice boomed in his ear. What Kim and Cullen were doing was sinful. After watching the two of them making out, Morgan jumped up, shoved back his chair, and stormed out of the bar.

By the time he reached his apartment, he was enraged. He texted Kim: "Fooling around with a married man will send you straight to hell bitch."

Then he texted warning after warning, warning her of the dire consequences of her "sinful behavior." The next morning he awoke, hung over, but his rage unrelenting. When he checked his phone, a string of tweets and posts came up on social media about the game. But what got his attention was Kim's post: "Shared a few victory drinks, and now I'm the "Spawn of Satan." Check out these texts LMAO! She'd posted Morgan's messages, and the hundreds of comments and replies set Morgan off even more!

Morgan got fired up when he read someone asked Kim who'd sent them, and Kim posted his name for the world to see! There were hundreds of comments back and forth making it obvious everyone thought he was a religious nut or worse. Many even called him a stalker! People advised Kim to stay away from him, and to block him!

Before she did, he was going to set the record straight. And although the messages and Kim's tone were hurtful, she was paying more attention to him than she ever had before. Morgan rejoiced in that. He defended himself and pointed out that the kisses went well past the bounds of respectability. A short while later, Kim wrote: "Blocked the creepy stalker bastard and plan to keep my distance."

Furious, Morgan set up a new social identity and sent Kim a friend request. When she accepted, he claimed to be a married man who'd read her previous posts and made lewd suggestions. Each time Kim blocked him, he assumed a different name and continued to harass her.

Kim's Solutions

When someone messages or posts something offensive don't delay. Act immediately. Start by taking a screenshot or printing out the messages, then block and report.

One random, cruel message may be nothing, but more than one or a string of messages warrants and immediate response – take action!

First of all, if anyone sends you more than one message that seems "off," even threatening, block that person right away, and report the messages to the administration of the social media platform and alert your network of the "happenings."

Watch out for new friend requests soon after you've blocked someone. They may assume a false identity the way Morgan did, intending to cyberstalk you again. Check all your social media accounts. If someone is using one means to send or post nasty messages, chances are they'll post to your other accounts as well. If you haven't already done so, reset all of your privacy settings to allow only friends to see your posts and to follow you.

CHAPTER 11

Dean's Story

Dean met Shena during college orientation. Both psychology majors, they hit it off right away and soon became an item. Dean found Shena's brilliant mind, her sexy body, and her quick wit compelling. They had fun together. However, a darker side to her personality emerged soon after they got exclusive. It began when they were walking across campus, and Dean smiled and greeted a girl from one of their classes.

Shena quizzed him about how well he knew the girl. She kept badgering him, even when he said he was only friendly because he recognized her face from class. He greeted guys from the class too. But Shena wasn't satisfied. Whenever they were out, and Dean even glanced at a passing female, Shena accused him of being a "perv." One day a sociology classmate who was ill texted to ask about their homework, and Shena went ballistic, insisting he was sleeping with the girl.

Early in the relationship, Dean believed Shena's jealous streak showed how much she loved him, but as time went on, the accusations increased. It got to the point he couldn't even walk past another female without rousing Shena's suspicions. She even followed him to his job as a server in a restaurant, positive he was cheating on her with coworkers. If he didn't exit the restaurant immediately after closing, she peered through the glass or banged on the door until he came out.

After graduation, Dean was offered a job as a counselor at a local outpatient clinic. He decided to take the position in spite of Shena's temper fits. When she gave him an ultimatum – marry her and find another job – Dean refused, leading to a tumultuous breakup. Shena wasn't ready to let go, though. Several months later, Dean began dating a coworker, Lily. Wherever he went, restaurants, sporting events, and even the grocery store, Shena showed up. She sat near him and Lily in the movies, at concerts, and in bars. Dean thought the sightings were a coincidence, but as they happened more frequently, he became concerned. Especially when he spotted Shena driving by Lily's parent's house, an hour away from their hometown, he knew he needed to take action.

He went to his hometown police and reported the problem. Unfortunately, Shena had been there before him. She'd told the police that he'd been stalking her, and they had records of several complaints against him.

After he and Lily had announced their engagement, the situation worsened. Shena hacked into Dean's wireless account and sent messages to all of his contacts claiming he was a cheating bastard.

Shortly after that, Dean discovered that Shena had installed spyware on his computer and was reading his emails. In fact, she'd been tracking him online for years after sending him an e-card every birthday with spyware attached. Dean kept all his appointments in his online calendar that was synced up with his phone and tablet, which explained how she knew his whereabouts all the time.
Complaints to the local police resulted in accusations that he was the stalker and a cyberstalker. As more reports got

filed against him, and with nowhere else to turn, he looked for someone that could help him. Being a male reporting the instances of cyberstalking and stalking posed a problem.

Dean could feel right away that when he reported to law enforcement, they didn't believe him. They quizzed him and made him feel like he was in the wrong and should not be reporting. He heard one officer tell another in fact "we got the perp right here reporting."

Dean's Solution

Dean reached out, mortified because he understood that law enforcement believed he was the predator and had not taken his reports of cyberstalking and stalking seriously at all.

I had Dean keep an "Events Time Line," with the following headings: **DATE, TIME, INCIDENT, and EVIDENCE.**

The final column was especially important because the police didn't believe Dean's reports. He asked friends, family members, and sometimes even random strangers to report the incidents and include their contact information so the police could contact them. Doing this added credibility to his story and I had hoped that with time, it would be sufficient to garner their support. No one deserves to live or work in fear!

Not everyone was willing to verify the information, but some, such as a bartender at his favorite bar and a clerk at the local mini- mart had seen Shena standing around waiting for him numerous times. They were willing to vouch that she'd been stalking him. Dean compiled a long list to provide to the authorities.

I had advised him that stalking and cyberstalking required many repeated instances before they were taken seriously, even when there is a female victim reporting.

Some jurisdictions require that there be threats of violence, others more than that, and label the instances of cyberstalking as

ID theft, or a part thereof. Therefore, patience is required as well as being very proactive, because there was no telling what Shena was going to do next and she could be potentially dangerous.

Luckily, in Dean's case, his complaints were taken seriously. I contacted a prosecutor in the stalking unit that I knew from prior training. She helped Dean get his report taken and sent to the city attorney for review and the charges filed.

He and Lily were relieved to discover they had a strong case against Shena. They had been recording the instances in their journal, **"The Events Time Line"** and had compiled a strong, comprehensive witness list that made the case more powerful against Shena.

Dean filed a restraining order, and Shena was ordered not to contact Dean or Lily by phone, or by use of electronic means. She was also not allowed to come within one hundred yards of them. Restraining orders will not stop all predators, but in Shena's case, she did not want to risk getting caught, so she stopped her cyberabuse and stalking.

Self-Help Action Steps

• Have all of your electronic devices checked for spyware and viruses. Take all of your electronic devices to a tech pro and have them analyze them. It's a good practice even if you are not experiencing cyberstalking or stalking.
• Use what is available to create your safety plan and to gather evidence. Dean knew which gas stations had cameras pointed at the pump. He also knew what stores and parking lots had video surveillance and used that to his advantage. Do the same.
• If followed by a car, remain calm, phone for help, then pull into the local police station, fire department, or hospital emergency room parking area. They are open 24/7.

- Use Uber, Lyft, Taxi and ride share as often as you can when traveling by car.

- Be vigilantly alert when in public and vary your routine to prevent the stalker from tracking you. Take different routes to school, to work, to the gym, etc. Stalkers like easy "prey." Do not make it easy for them!

- Warn family, friends, classmates, and coworkers. By warning them, you will prevent the possibility of them inadvertently giving out information about your activities and whereabouts to the stalker.

- Home video surveillance systems are fairly inexpensive. Often you can rent a system. Get one installed in your home and for your car.

All of these **"Self-Help Action Steps"** are to help avoid the proverbial "he said, she said." Far too often, it is the reason why stalking cases fail to get investigated, or charges filed.

The majority of stalking cases are difficult to prosecute because the victims fail to have sufficient evidence to support making an arrest. Sadly, many victims do not find help and end up being a "stalking homicide." Don't let this happen to you or to someone you love!

CHAPTER 12

Sonny's Story

Sonny is an attractive comedian and TV personality and is accustomed to having fans gush over him in his hometown. When he went out shopping, people sometimes stopped him for autographs or asked if they could snap a selfie with him.

Inside he was secretly pleased with being recognized and always obliged, to keep the public happy. He also enjoyed getting fan mail and complimentary comments whenever he posted excerpts of his act online.

The SUPERFAN

There was a woman, who went by the name of "KewlKitty," who responded to every post he wrote. She also commented on each show's announcement and the social sites. At first, the remarks were general: "good job," "hilarious" or "great gig." Over time, her compliments grew more unrestrained, and Sonny enjoyed her praise.

It was nice to perform and draw in a supportive response, and he looked forward to seeing how his "superfan" would respond to each new act he performed. That was, until "KewlKitty's" remarks became personal. They progressed from, "You are the greatest! I love what you do!" or, "Sonny, you are so freaking hot...Meow! I watch every show!"

It appeared to others that they had a connection outside of work, and at times her comments almost seemed as if he had been following her. He felt a bit nervous and at times very uncomfortable, but shook off the bad feelings, rationalizing that it was a fairly small town and perhaps she'd seen him out and about.

Sonny concentrated on getting his lines together for his next show, and it just so happened that in the headlines he had heard about a cyberstalking case and Survivors in Action. He contacted me for some information. At first contact, he said he was reaching out for a "friend" experiencing something, and he wasn't sure if it was cyberstalking.

As he and I talked, Sonny's uneasiness increased. Many of the early warning signs of cyberstalking that I mentioned matched his situation, but being a macho guy and a comedian he made light of it and was too embarrassed to confess that he was the victim.

Trust Your Gut

After he had got off the phone, Sonny started to worry. The more he looked at his notes, the more obvious it became he'd been dismissing a situation that might be a potential cyberstalking scenario. One of the things I had stressed was paying attention to gut feelings. "If something feels off to you, it probably is," I had said.

If Sonny was honest, his gut had been warning him for months now, but dudes don't report cyberstalking, and he was a comedian and didn't want to be a victim. It was funny even to him. He wrote a line about it for his act even.

His fears increased when KewlKitty called the club he was performing at and asked to speak with him. The call was passed on to him because she claimed to be a close friend.

Next, she sent him a text. The club's number was public, but this gal had managed to get his cell number. The texts were explicit and, they revealed that she knew private details of his life, including where he lived. The text that disturbed him the most was when she said she had plans to meet him in person soon – real soon.

Sonny called me with the pretext of offering me free show tickets, but he gradually brought the conversation around to his real reason for calling. The minute I heard the story, I confirmed that he needed to act immediately to protect himself from a cyberstalker and potential stalker who could be dangerous.

Sonny's Solution

Maintaining a different persona for on-stage and off-stage might mean that fewer fans would recognize him when he was out, but at this point, he was more concerned with safety than stardom. And unless he started varying his appearance, it would be hard to disguise himself in his hometown.

A superfan can happen to anyone! With the power of social media sites, most of us are the stars of our own reality show. We post daily the most intimate details of our lives publicly, (such as where we go, who we are dating, what we eat, how we vote), we are opening ourselves to the possibility.

Staying Safe

The other thing I stressed, especially if someone was following him, was for Sonny to vary his routes to and from the grocery store, gym and anywhere else he went consistently. I suggested for him to keep a routine that was slightly varied. Being unpredictable throws off stalkers and makes it easier to spot them.

Sonny's friends all wanted him to join in with them practicing martial arts, so he took them up on it and made this part of his exercise routine. Making jokes that he was "Sonny the Super Ninja" as part of his act, and showing off a skill or two he acquired while training was powerful for him.

Protecting Personal Information

Opening a private mailbox at the local UPS Store adds one more layer of protection against unwanted advances.

Opening a wireless account in a business name, and using a business tax identification number (TIN) instead of his social security number made a difference. These were simple to effectuate, and good privacy mechanisms to help shield him.

Letting his friends and family know about the problem also made a difference. His colleagues in comedy made light of the ordeal, in fact, he was even labeled the "guy with the stalker," but now they, as well as friends, and relatives, stay aware and alert to signs of a stalker. They also knew not to respond if someone contacted them for information about him.

I also recommended having a "bat phone." This secret prepaid cell phone is for making plans, contacting relatives and best friends, or reporting emergencies. It offers peace of mind to know that if the phone rang, it would only be people he knew. He could silence his other phones or even leave his regular cell phone behind without comprising his security.

VOIP (Voice Over Internet Phone), Voice Over Internet Protocol, or in more common terms phone service over the Internet, are powerful tools also, and often no cost ways to make and receive calls that add privacy safeguard in stalking and cyberabuse situations. Many businesses these days operate strictly using VOIP systems even - they are increasingly popular and easy to use.

Whatever method works best for you. Be open to trying any method or variation herein. Self-help advocacy is a trial and error approach. Be patient and find what methods work best for you and your situation, and keep a record on your **"Events Time Line."**

CHAPTER 13

Megan's Story

    Megan didn't realize that shy, geeky Emily was obsessed with her. Emily followed her in the halls, watched her every move, and tried to imitate her. Emily dyed her black hair blonde like Megan's and bought similar clothes and shoes. When Megan's friends giggled about her clone, Megan finally noticed. It was annoying to have someone copying her every move, but Megan brushed it off. Emily was obviously insecure and trying hard to become popular. In fact, Megan was even flattered until the day she was alone in a room with Emily after school.

    The rest of the school newspaper staff had left, but Megan was still editing her article. As usual, Emily sat the desk behind her. Head bent over her work, Megan flipped her long blonde hair back out of her way. Suddenly, her head jerked back as Emily grabbed a fistful of hair. Before Megan could yank away, Emily hacked off a huge chunk of her hair. Interestingly enough, in this case, Emily hadn't done it out of jealousy or for revenge. When confronted, she tearfully admitted that she only wanted to have something special of Megan's. She had other things as well, such as, a few of Megan's, old hair ties and lip gloss that she had taken from Megan's bag while it hung on the back of her chair. She followed Megan online and memorized some of the quotes from Megan's posts. Emily planned to add the hair to her Megan collection.

Emily had been so obsessed   that she hadn't considered the consequences of her actions. In many cases incidents like these lead to cyberabuse and stalking, as they did with Jake, a rugby star, attending an all-boys religious school.

CHAPTER 14

Jake's Story

After a semi-final game at a rival school, the team members left their sports bags and equipment in the hallway, while they waited for the bus. A group of girls from the other school joined them at the stadium concession stand and flirted with all the players, especially Jake, who was not only an outstanding athlete, but also extremely handsome. One girl, in particular, cozied up to him. So much so, he felt uncomfortable. He'd seen her in the stands at all his games, and she'd wait for him after every game to tell him how awesome he'd played.

Jake had a girlfriend from his hometown, and he was shy, so he edged away whenever she invaded his personal space. He was too tongue-tied to discourage her advances, so this particular night, he was relieved when she excused herself to use the restroom. As soon as she was out of sight, he wedged his chair between two of his teammates' seats, leaving no room for her.

Amy's disappointment was obvious when she returned. Still, she kept flashing him smiles as if they shared a secret. Jake was grateful when the bus pulled up. She inched up to him and asked for his number, but he pretended not to hear and hurried up the bus steps. Amy wrangled numbers from several of his teammates and promised to keep in touch. As the bus pulled away, she blew him kisses, prompting several teammates to remark, "Dude that girl's got the hots for you."

In the locker room, Jake couldn't find his practice jersey. He shrugged assuming someone else picked it up and tossed it into the communal laundry pile, and he'd have it for the next game.
Two days later Amy texted: "Missing anything?" She attached a picture of herself in his jersey, lying on a rumpled bed, hair mussed, legs spread, and with no panties on.

Jake's face burned when he saw she'd sent it to several teammates.
"Remember this? We had fun, didn't we?" She wrote next, accompanied by more lewd pictures. Each message made it sound as if they'd been together.

Sick to his stomach, Jake blocked her number, but he couldn't erase the pictures from his mind. The photos quickly made the rounds at school. A few classmates made comments or congratulated him. One student, jealous of Jake anonymously reported him to the dean.

No matter how much Jake protested his innocence, his classmates didn't believe him. Neither did the school disciplinary committee. Again and again, they doubted his claim that the jersey was stolen and questioned why he hadn't reported it. They pressured him to confess to his sin and to stop lying about it.

When he clammed up and shook his head, they suspended him. His coach and teammates were upset. His girlfriend called in tears wanting to break up. Even his parents looked at him skeptically. Alone in his room the night of the championship game, Jake questioned why God had let this happen. A few weeks ago, he'd been an honor student headed to a prestigious college on a rugby scholarship. Now he'd lost it all. Suicide seemed his only option. Although he struggled with doubt, in the end, his faith stopped him from pulling the trigger.

Jake's Solution

A private investigator and a local attorney who were friends of Jake's father had learned of Jake's situation and took on the case pro bono. The investigator went to Amy's school to interview students, many of whom had heard Amy's bragging about stealing the jersey. One of Jake's teammates confessed he'd given Jake's phone number to Amy when she'd begged for it. He still had the text message.

After collecting statements from the students and other witnesses, such as the coaches and teammates who'd seen Amy stalking Jake after games, the investigator contacted school officials with the information. She convinced them that Jake had not given Amy the jersey nor had he been seeing the girl.

When confronted, Amy admitted that she'd had no contact with Jake except in the presence of others. The headmaster at her school insisted she write a letter of apology to Jake and that she stay away from his sporting events. Jake's school extended an official apology, reinstated him with all his previous honors, and to avoid a possible lawsuit; they waived his tuition for the remainder of the school year. Because of their religious beliefs, filing charges against Amy did not happen.

Physical Safety Tips

In addition to following the same steps Sonny did, such as varying your routine, walking with others, learning self-defense, and carrying a prepaid phone, always park in well-lit areas and consider your safety first and foremost. Know your area and select safe zones in the off chance that you need to get away, or fear someone is following you. Find places with video cameras and 24-hour security. Head for these safe zones while you dial 911, or stand there to gather your wits until you can determine if you have a threat.

Sonny knew the coffee shops on the north, and east corners of his block both had video surveillance and the bank a few doors away had an armed security guard 24/7. Rather than using the ATM that was not as secure, he went to the nearby bank, where he could stand in a lighted area and attract the guard's attention if he had problems. He chose a gas station with 24-hour video surveillance as a safe zone to buy gas. The cameras would document the situation if someone were following him while driving.

SIA also helped Sonny create a safety plan that listed his **Self-Help Action Steps:**

• If he was followed or had a stalker confrontation at home, or while driving, follow the safety steps listed above. These safety plans are not complicated. They are simple steps to take in an emergency situation. Become familiar with and rehearse the plans regularly. Be sure to update the plans when changing jobs, traveling out of town, attending classes, appearing at an event, or visiting a foreign country.

• For added protection, contact a personal safety protection expert. Usually, one or two consultations will provide enough information to create a safety plan and avoid violence. Some consultants discount their rates if the client goes to a class sponsored by a non-profit.

• Private investigators and risk management consultants are also helpful because they are familiar with the legal system and can provide support to help garner law enforcement attention, restraining orders, and successful prosecution.

• In some situations, stalking victims choose to carry a handheld alarm, pepper spray, stun gun or a weapon.

• Familiarize yourself with the state laws and obtain the proper training and permits. Observe all cautions when using any weapon, and remember that your own firearm could easily be used against you, so learn to protect yourself in these situations.

Home Safety Tips

Consider installing security cameras at home. These are becoming less and less expensive, and many security companies will offer rental programs. It may be possible to get them at a discount or even donated if you're working with a non-profit group.

As a temporary measure, find something that looks like a camera and put it in your window. Most stalkers won't risk getting close enough to tell it's fake.

One man bought fake security cameras and installed them at his door and outside the exterior of his home and office. The flashing red light on the bottom of the cameras even fooled a police officer who came out to investigate his report of a stalker. Actual protection is better than trying to fool stalkers, but these tricks may help deter predators until the real thing is set up.

When you consult with security companies, ask for their recommendations for protecting your home and property. Don't be afraid to say you have a stalking situation.

Phone and Online Safety Tips

Use an answering service, a booking agent or have all unknown incoming calls go to voice mail.

Some of my clients who own businesses and can't afford a service and don't want to miss calls, forward their calls to house- bound relatives, or volunteers that are part of the **Survivors in Action network.**

It's amazing how putting a senior to work answering the phone gives them a sense of purpose and fulfillment that they otherwise wouldn't have. Be creative. Find a solution that works, so that you stay in control and don't have to waste precious time away from living a full life!

Use the electronic voice mail on your wireless phone or have someone else record the message on your voice mail. Stalkers like to hear the voice of their victims to feel close to them and maintain their illusion of a relationship or love affair. Although it's false, they thrive on the feeling of connection. Hearing your voice or seeing your response empowers them and feeds their fantasies. If they can't hear you or can't get directly to you, they may seek out another victim they can reach.

Avoid publishing information online regarding your personal life or day-to-day activities without first considering the outcome. Never mention names of family members or friends as they may end up getting stalked too. Stalkers have shown up at schools that the victims attend. They frequent the victim's favorite restaurant or join and attend the same civic clubs and events.

Be careful not to use logins, passwords, or security questions that relate to your interests. Personal profiles and bios contain so much personal information these days that they reveal everything from your favorite colors and foods to the names of your significant other, children, relatives, and pets. Birthdates, graduations, anniversaries, and other data are readily available to stalkers!

They can look up places where you've lived, parents' names, and other information typically chosen as answers to security questions. Rather than using answers that may be public knowledge, try to find creative answers to the questions. But always choose answers you'll remember, or write them down and keep them in a safe place.

Web counters on your sites can record incoming IP addresses, city, state, time, and duration. Monitor these for spikes in activity from a certain area or computer. Keep logs of IP addresses of frequent commenters. Record all incoming calls to your work number as well. Documentation is of key importance.

If you suspect you have a stalker, it might be wise to throw in false clues to your whereabouts and plans on social media. Be creative in what you share. It's better to share information about events after they've occurred rather than before they happen. Satisfy your followers with post-event pictures rather than revealing your excitement leading up to the activity.

It's become much harder maintain privacy. Internet sites offer personal information, including addresses, phone numbers, and names of significant others. Any stalker, with a little investment of money and time, can find out where his/her target lives.

Quick Tips

- Protect private information

- Direct all unknown incoming calls to voicemail or forward to a 3rd party.

- Use a mail drop or post office box for additional privacy.

- Never share information about your home or family

- Get a "bat phone" or VOIP line to stay in touch with those closest to you.

- Vary routines and document.

- Keep an "Events Time Line."

- Use Uber, Lyft, Taxi and ride share as often as you can when traveling by car.

CHAPTER 15

Casey and Monica's Story

Casey was separated, and his divorce finalized soon. His divorce was tumultuous, and he had constant problems with his soon to be ex-wife Anita always wanting to change the already agreed upon terms of their settlement. Her demands seemed to be constant and never ending. He was in and out of his lawyer's office trying to find a way to settle it and move on.

In fact, Casey had already moved on. He was now living with his girlfriend Monica, which angered his former spouse Anita even more! She didn't want Casey to move on and even told her attorney and Casey in person on many occasions that "they were going to get back together."

She had the sick twisted belief that somehow she and Casey were going to be together and was keeping Casey's last name even just to spite him.

They had no children, and the assets they did have, Casey wanted to divide with her equally so that he could move along with his life. Anita was miserable. She hadn't met anyone yet and focused on finding ways to stall the settlement and keep Casey in her life.

She had tried everything in her power so far to get him back. She contacted his mother and sister and often would send him text messages saying the two of them should get back together.

Casey didn't want to inflame her more, so on the advice of his attorney, he acted as if the "cat never scratched," never responding to her texts or to her constant pleas to get back together.

He kept his cool and thought that with time she would stop. Casey was a bit naïve too. He had fallen madly in love with Monica, and she was the focus of his life.

Casey and Monica were happy. The pair started a successful clothing business together and were looking to expand shortly. Neither of them was particularly tech savvy. Monica worked in retail and sales most of her life and hadn't needed to rely upon the computer, except for doing accounting and sending the basic email or two.

Like Monica, Casey was also in sales, and he relied on banking apps to make his life easier. On the advice of his CPA, he enrolled in online banking, setting up his account to pay his bills every month, so that way he wouldn't forget and then have to pay those dreaded late fees. He was spending so much time with Monica and running their clothing business that he had often got distracted and would forget to pay his bills on time.

He signed up to receive alerts if his bank balance was lower than $500, and had received a text that caused him to stop short: "This is a Chase Low Balance Alert."

Casey didn't know why he was receiving this message. He hadn't withdrawn any funds and always had a nest egg in his account for what he called the "rainy day fund." It was just in case that old Mercedes needed another something because every repair bill was at least $500.00.

Nevertheless, he thought perhaps Monica had made a large purchase at a clothing show she was attending, and he would log in to see what this was all about in a minute or two after he made the bank deposit.

But then the worst happened.

Casey snapped a picture, made his deposit and logged in to his account to check things out. The account balance didn't make sense. There were at least six pending charges, and none of them were for wholesale clothing. They were for his bills that he had just paid weeks earlier. He wanted to investigate, so he contacted the bank and logged in online and started a chat session with customer service.

When he logged into his banking app, he could see that the bills he had paid weeks earlier, were paid again. There was no reason for this to happen. He didn't authorize any new "one time payments."

At first glance, he wrote it off as a banking glitch. Then he contacted the bank to let them know that this had happened so that "they could get it cleared up." Little did he know that this was not the case!

As it turned out, his soon to be ex-wife Anita, armed with all of his information including social security number, mother's maiden name and the passwords for all of his accounts, logged in to his account and scheduled one-time bill payments. That is what threw his entire account into overdraft status.

His monthly mortgage payment was made "again" wirelessly, as were student loan payments, auto insurance, recurring credit card payments, and store lease payments, all had been made again, "one time." It appeared that he made the payments.

A person, in this case, a cyberstalker, using an electronic device phone, pad, or other tech device utilized the victims known personal and banking information and scheduled bill payments electronically. Often, this is a practice utilized by cyberstalkers who are intimately known to the victims.

Frequently, this happens in cases involving divorce proceedings, or where intimate partners or business partners separate.
In Casey's situation, he was going through a nasty divorce. His lawyer and the court papers he received, never advised him about cyberstalking or the potential that something like this could happen. He had moved on with his life and hadn't thought for a second that anything like this could happen.

It's is not something that's taught in law school, so no blaming Casey's lawyer. There is also no reason to blame the bank or for that matter, the banking apps. The technological tools have been created long before the inception of cyberstalking, and the potential conduct of cyberstalkers using tech to stalk wasn't considered or factored in when the app or automatic bill pay feature was created.

All of these applications, the "tech time-saving tools" of today with their convenient online features, have all evolved with the convenience of the user and the banking institution in mind, not with the mindset that a cyberstalker was going to use them.

Casey's Solution

In Casey's situation, paying the bills earlier, it caused his overdraft protection to be activated, so he wasn't out any service fees or overdraft charges. He found out the hard way, how difficult it was to "re-ring the bell" after it was already rung so to speak.

Getting credit back for the mortgage payment that had been paid ahead, as well as the early credit card payments and student loan payments was impossible without being willing to spend endless hours on the phone and writing letter after letter and completing form after form.

It was evident early on, that long before the process of getting the money credited back into his account would take place, the next months' bills would be due.

Casey took the hit, and had less cash in his "rainy day fund," but immediately set up new passwords and opened a new bank account to prevent this cyberabuse from happening again.

In Casey's case, the bank customer service department's first response was to advise him that he "must have inadvertently hit the wrong button, therefore paying his bills without realizing it."
Casey was extremely frustrated during his chat session with the bank's customer service department.

The response, "accidents do happen," and "I see that your bills were scheduled for one-time payment, I am pleased to confirm," were being texted to him via the chat he had opened with the bank. When he insisted he had not scheduled the payments, he was then told to contact security to report the identity theft.

The chat messages back and forth between Casey and the customer service representatives were all singing the same tune, "You did this by accident." Some even said, "This is a good thing because you are paying on time."

Casey, enraged by the chat session and the customer service representatives, needed to place the blame on someone. He wanted to blame someone but had never thought to blame his ex-wife, so he lashed out on the person closest to him, Monica.
He called up Monica furious, and when she didn't answer, he texted her one after the other that she better call him and that her fuck up was bullshit!

Monica, not knowing what was going on texted him back, "WTF?" She left the wholesaler where she was buying new inventory for their store and called him back.

After he had explained what was happening, she realized he was upset, and she explained she hadn't done anything and was submitting purchase orders that required no deposit, so it wasn't her that scheduled the payments.

Casey never thought about his ex-wife being a cyberstalker, and never thought about something like this happening. They were no longer living together. They had separated for over a year.

It wasn't identity theft. No one had stolen Casey's money, and it was not an accident. He didn't pay his bills early, nor did Monica do anything, so what was going on?

Cyberabuse. Specifically, it was cyberstalking. What had happened to Casey had happened to me in the past, and was part of many news articles published on the topic of cyberstalking.

Shortly afterward, Monica was sitting under the dryer while getting her hair done and picked up a magazine to read. She discovered an article published about me and my work helping cyberstalking victims. She contacted **Survivors in Action**.

What happened to Casey has happened to many others. Many write off the payments as computer glitches and don't even realize that there was a sinister cyberstalker behind until much later down the line when they finally put two and two together!

My story didn't have the happy ending like Casey. I didn't have the "rainy day funds" saved aside to be able to not suffer from the cyberstalkers sinister actions. I was an abuse survivor starting over with nothing but the clothes on my back. I was trying to start over, with a vicious stalker and cyberstalker on my tail.

Casey and Monica changed all of their passwords and opened new bank accounts. They no longer used old personal identifiers from their past either.

Along the way it was discovered that Monica had stored a document on her tablet labeled; "Monica and Casey Password." It contained all of their information including bank accounts, investment information, as well as their online passwords to his and her accounts. It was all stored and easy to be found by anyone. The file was removed and stored elsewhere, safely hidden out of a cyberstalker's or identity thief's reach.

Self-Help Action Steps:

- Delete the document with account passwords and information from all computers. Do not store them in a computer.

- Report to law enforcement and "create the public safety paper trail" so that if the behavior escalates, you have documentation.

- Open new bank accounts, new investment accounts, new wireless accounts using new identifiers and start fresh.

- After returning to banking online, change passwords monthly.

- Double check to be sure that the password retrieval email is your email rather than someone else's.

- Change all security questions to make sure the answers are very difficult and not ones the cyberstalker can easily figure out.

Other Strategies

Additional Precautions for Banking or Monetary Fraud

Once you've secured your accounts with the strategies Casey and Monica used, it's important to prevent cyberstalking from happening again.

- Phone the three national credit bureaus to place a credit freeze and fraud alert on your credit reports. Request that all creditors contact consumer before issuing any new lines of credit or banking accounts or making changes to existing accounts.

- Complete an affidavit of forgery and have it notarized for any account opened without your consent or permission.

- Check your credit bureau information at least twice a year and pay close attention to the online activity.

CHAPTER 16

Lara's Story

Lara had been dating Kurtis. They had fun whenever they weren't busy with work. Time off together was filled with boating and partying.

Kurtis and a best friend started their computer tech company. To get it off the ground, he worked long hours, often until the wee hours of the morning and most weekends. Lara, who had been working as a contract paralegal, was thrilled to be offered a full-time job when one of the paralegals retired at the law firm she was working.

Soon, she too was spending long hours researching case law, doing client intake, and overseeing the legal assistants and calendaring at the fairly large law firm where she worked. She and Kurtis rarely saw each other.

Both of them were so stressed out by their jobs, that when they did have time together, they often ended up fighting. Many of their arguments began with Kurtis accusing Lara of spending more time with her friends or on her work than with him. Whenever he was home, he expected her to drop everything to pay attention to him. His attitude was that he deserved down time after working long hours, and her needs could wait.

The longer they were together, the more demanding Kurtis became. He decided what they watched on TV, where they went, what they ate, and who they saw. He was also more and more demanding in the bedroom. She didn't want to lose him. She also rationalized that he was working much longer hours than she was, so it was only fair for things to go his way when he was home.

But when Kurtis ordered her not to see her best friend Kate because he considered her a bad influence, and to discontinue the wireless plan on her telephone because it cost too much, Lara balked. Defying him, she texted and went out with friends anyway, and when Kurtis wasn't home, she took the boat out. She had learned at an early age how to be a "captain of her life." Her mom, a retired Navy captain, taught her plenty, and she had been driving and operating the family 28-foot ski boat since she was in the 3rd grade. She wasn't going to let him stop her!

When he discovered she hadn't listened, he threw a fit. Usually, Lara gave in, but this time she didn't. She stomped off and locked herself in the bathroom. A short while later Kurtis banged on the door.

This pattern continued most weekends, with Kurtis becoming more controlling and demanding. When he didn't get his way, he lost his temper and often made her pay for resisting his directives with cruel cutting remarks or doing things he knew would hurt or make her uncomfortable.

He became more and more demanding sexually. He wanted to record their lovemaking with the idea that he wanted to "enjoy it" while he was at work, and when they were apart. Lara reluctantly agreed, thinking that perhaps it may make the relationship stronger, and get Kurtis to come around about her interactions with friends and family. She wanted to ease the tension and keep the peace.

Escaping the Pain

One Saturday after Kurtis had taped Lara and him having sex, they had a bad fight. Lara called Kate, who had been encouraging her to leave Kurtis all along. Kate offered to let Lara stay at her apartment. Relieved, Lara packed her car as soon as Kurtis left for work. She didn't know how long she'd stay, so she took most of her things.

With tears streaming down her face, Lara drove to Kate's apartment, where her friend greeted her with open arms. To cheer Lara up, Kate suggested going out to their favorite bar that evening. They unpacked the car and then got ready for their night out on the town. Lara was still feeling off and uncertain about her relationship with Kurtis, but she was determined to put him out of her mind for a while and enjoy herself.

The pair had fun and posted a few selfies all dolled up and ready for a girl's night out on the town.

Night Out, Gone Bad

As she and Kate joked and laughed like old times, Lara relaxed. After a few cocktails and some great belly laughs, she had put the Kurtis situation out of her mind. She was sure she'd made the right decision to leave Kurtis. She was feeling happier than she had in a long time.

She excused herself to go to the restroom and had no sooner locked herself in a stall when a woman entered the restroom chattering on her cell phone. "Yes, I got the pictures. How disgusting. She's a paralegal at Lee and Edison isn't she?" The woman practically screeched, "Who would want someone like that working at the firm?"

Lara was working at Lee and Edison a fairly large law practice in the area in the town of Lakewood. She remained in the stall and eavesdropped, hoping to hear more.

The woman continued to rant. "You see it in the news all the time! Women who use their bodies for such despicable reasons and will do anything to advance their careers are disgusting and repulsive! And we have this Lara Williams right in our community too. Someone should report her to the police."

Lara gasped. She rushed from the stall, demanding to know what the woman was speaking about.

The woman's eyes widened, and her cheeks reddened, but her face screwed up into an expression of distaste. "Posting obscene pictures of yourself on the Internet. You're disgusting."

Lara stood there in shock. Then the restroom door banged open, and Kate rushed in. She dragged Lara out the door, while people stared and snickered as they passed. In the car, Kate handed Lara her phone.

No One Leaves Me

There were pictures of Lara naked in suggestive and lewd poses, and the videos of her and Kurtis were everywhere! What had been private moments that were captured to keep the peace in their relationship, were now threatening to ruin her entire life!

All of the intimate moments together that Kurtis had videotaped and recorded during their relationship along with other images, some that he had obviously photo-shopped were there.

Lara's cheeks burned when she saw that the pictures had been sent from her account to every person on her email list, including coworkers, partners at the law firm, her mother, her minister and even some clients at the firm.

"Shit, shit, shit, this is not good!" she said aloud to herself. Her heart sank into the pit of her stomach.

She checked her phone and found messages from people expressing shock and disgust. There was hate mail, lewd responses, and twenty-two texts from Kurtis. Every one of them said the same thing: "No one leaves me."

Even worse, the pictures had gone viral. People were forwarding her pictures and videos under huge bold headings, "Lara Williams is a slut." For all she knew, Kurtis had done that as well.

Lara buried her head in her hands. What was she going to do? She could never show up in public again, and she'd never been able to go back to work at the firm.

Even if the partners let her through the door, how could she face all of them? The partners, associates, law clerks, legal assistants, and other paralegals, had all seen her naked and having sex!

Lara's Solution

During their relationship, Lara had recognized Kurtis's need to control. He demanded to know her passwords and private information, but she loved him and gave him whatever he asked for, including free access to record all of their most private and intimate moments. He had taken videos of them having sex; she had sent him pictures of herself naked, and in suggestive postures. It was private and what she thought would be helpful to building and maintaining their relationship. She loved Kurtis and never thought of what could happen.

Because Lara's decision to leave Kurtis happened suddenly, she had little time to plan for her protection. In fact, she didn't even consider the possibility that he'd try to hurt her. If she'd paid more attention to how he reacted when she did things he forbid her to do, she might have prepared for his cruelty after the breakup. But because she'd never dream of hurting someone who broke up with her, it didn't occur to her that she'd need to protect herself.

Although she couldn't stop the spread of the pictures or videos much less erase them from people's memories, she wanted to mitigate some of the harm they'd done.

Kate, a witty one started the damage control by hitting "Reply All," and typing "LOL. I can't believe your ex was stupid enough to think people would believe these pictures are of you. Anyone with any brains can see they've been photo-shopped. What a loser!" Then Kate attached a close-up of the neck of one of the altered pictures where it was obvious someone's head had was attached to another body.

Then Kate's mom also sent out a supportive email that went to everyone on the list. "Honey, I told you that Kurtis was trouble. I'm so sorry you had to find out this way."

Another girlfriend wrote: "You poor thing. I dated that bastard Kurtis Livingston, and you wouldn't believe the nasty things he did to me when we broke up."

A high school friend wrote: "Kurtis Livingston? The one who graduated from Lakewood High with us? Figures he'd be behind this. He was always a sneaky SOB."

They sent out these emails as if they'd accidentally hit "reply all." They counted on people being curious or voyeuristic and reading Lara's "private" emails. The goal of the emails was to change people's attitudes from censoring Lara to sympathizing with her, and to focus people's attention away from the pictures and the sex videos.

In addition to the four people Lara recruited to send messages, several other people chimed in, mentioning things Kurtis had done. It hadn't been Lara's intent to bash Kurtis; she'd only wanted to let people know that she hadn't sent the emails and to focus people's attention away from the pictures. It seemed, though, as if Kurtis had hurt quite a few other people, judging from the emails flying around.

People sent emails to the partners at the law firm vouching for Lara's character and reputation. Friends, colleagues, and even several university professors made clear statements that Lara was not the kind of person those email images portrayed.

One of the partners of the firm contacted Lara privately to tell her that she and several others didn't care about the pictures and videos that were circulating. However, given the outcry from the other partners and the client's response, the partners would have no choice but to keep her on paid leave until it was all sorted out.

While she waited for the situation to resolve, Lara rarely went out because people sneered and jeered as she passed them on the sidewalk. The first time she entered the grocery store, people stopped and stared. Several men undressed her with their eyes; parents yanked their children away as if afraid she'd snatch them. The cashier recoiled from touching Lara's groceries. While she was in the store, someone spray painted the word slut on her car door. She returned from the grocery store in tears.

After that, Kate ran errands for her and brought her groceries, or they ordered them online and had them delivered. Kate was one of the few friends who stood by Lara. Work colleagues avoided her, and acquaintances who visited mainly came to ferret out gossip.

As time dragged on the paid leave period ended, now with no paychecks coming in, Lara couldn't pay her bills. Kate offered to let her stay rent free until things settled, but Lara hated imposing on her friend. She had little choice, though, unless she returned to Kurtis, the last thing she'd ever do.

She had agreed to deposit her paychecks into Kurtis's account. While they were together, he'd paid all the bills and given her weekly spending money. Anything they'd saved together was in his name. Now that they'd split, she had nothing. She had one charge card from her single days, but that was soon maxed out.

Lara was an emotional wreck. She avoided all her usual activities, and no one invited her to social events. She'd become a pariah in the community, and she had no idea if, or when her name would ever get cleared. While she was virtually a prisoner, Kurtis was roaming free, enjoying his victory.

Lara's Solution

Lara contacted **Survivors in Action.** By the time I had any involvement in her case, there were hundreds of postings of the videos online, the images and the smear campaign against her were ruining her life.

Laws and protections in place for victims of non-consensual pornography and cyberstalking were nearly non-existent then. While this was not making news headlines, what was making headlines was the imagery itself and the non-consensual pornography videos.
It was difficult to find anyone to support her. When she reached out for help, most were too busy doing net searches to see the videos and the images for themselves. Couple this with the public interest, the images and videos rocketed to the top of the search engines, making it even more difficult to make them disappear.

Lara was not going to settle with being named the town slut and having to hide for the rest of her life. She knew enough about the legal system to know she needed a lawyer but finding one that would take her case proved difficult.

The legal profession primarily being a male dominated one, made it more difficult for Lara. It was not easy explaining how these videos went viral and that she allowed Kurtis to tape them to injury lawyers.

The issue most lawyers argued was one of consent. They argued that she consented to these videos, so she had no recourse.

I was an advocate, not an attorney at the time. I told Lara, just as I have told many victims of cyberabuse, to counter back and argue with the lawyers that yes she consented, but that she didn't consent to have them go public and assimilated outside the privacy of her home.

Now, as an attorney, I understand that lawyers' opinions and interpretations of the law will vary from one to the other.

With all of this taken into account, just when I was about to quit law school for the hundredth time, I am thankful that my law professor always told me to "keep the faith" and paraphrasing here, "There is no such thing as a stronger case or a stronger argument. It is a matter of what the judge or the jury believes and decides."

I also understood from the onset while helping victims of what is labeled, "non-consensual pornography" and "cyberabuse," two things must happen. Societal norms of what is accepted or not in regards to sex and sexual activity must evolve, and so do the mindsets of victims (all of us) living in the cyber-era.

Firstly, what gets shared is going to be made public. That is the mindset that all of us have to keep in the back of our mind.
There should be no doubt in anyone's mind that privacy no longer exists.

If a video goes viral, or an image goes viral, it's awful. It's embarrassing, and it sucks big time, but how you respond is key.

The response is what the cyberpredators are seeking. They want for you to be ashamed, violated, punished and controlled by their deplorable behavior! I say don't let it control you! Don't waste time feeling shameful. Face it head on.

It shouldn't be the elephant in the room either. There is nothing gross or despicable about being in love and sharing images or private moments with an intimate partner. The shame, embarrassment, and ridicule need to transfer towards to the predator. It is the cyberpredator who took the private images and moments and shared them, violating a bond of loyalty and trust. That is where the focus of ALL of our attention should go!

Sex is something that no one should be shocked by or ashamed of. There is something morbid that hovers over "sex" and being "sexual," as if it is a deadly disease or something. If society reacted differently towards sex and became more focused on the behavior of the cyberpredator who posted the videos or the images, things would change. They need to feel the pain and to pay for violating that sacred trust.

Lara finally found a lawyer specializing in personal injury cases that would take her case. It took her lots of time, and she had to reveal the grueling details over and over with many lawyers before she found one that would accept her as a client and take her case.

He promised no guarantee of the outcome of her case but agreed to help Lara because he had young daughters and didn't want them going through what she was.

She never received the justice she thought she deserved, but Lara settled this matter, and she was satisfied with the outcome.

Lara knew she had been through all this for a reason, and she was determined to take action and do something to help others.

A short time later, after being reinstated at the firm, Lara was browsing the queries of Volunteer Match and noticed postings from Survivors in Action seeking volunteers, and it clicked that this was what she needed to do.

That was Lara's start. In addition to volunteering with SIA, Lara became a leader in her community by starting an anti- cyberabuse campaign. She also volunteered to be a speaker and help others impacted by cyberstalking, non-consensual pornography, and sex-tortion.

CHAPTER 17

Gavin's Story

Gavin completed his real estate training and landed a job with a large firm a few months before Tammy joined. On her first day, Tammy made a whirlwind entrance, one that attracted a great deal of attention from everyone in the office, particularly the males. With a business suit molded tightly to her curves and blouse that dipped low enough to reveal her impressive cleavage, Tammy breezed into the office greeting each person with a friendly smile, letting her hand linger on an arm or coat sleeve after she shook hands. Her voice dropped to sultry and seductive when she spoke to the men in the office. Other women might have been jealous, but Tammy turned her sweet Southern accent and charming manner their way too, complimenting each of them.

She loved making calls, connecting at social events, doing open houses, and promoting their team. Though most of the time her spiel made it appear as if she worked alone, Gavin shrugged it off. Tammy offered to redesign the sign and ad to include her picture, and Gavin was happy to let her. When the signs arrived, Gavin was startled to see that Tammy's name and picture were now prominent. His name was now far less prominent, taking up a small space in the lower corner. He gritted his teeth and tamped down his irritation. After all, Tammy's pretty face would attract more clients. Plus, he'd never liked seeing his cheesy smile in the ads. He also tried not to resent that she made herself the focus of attention at every client meeting and open house. Most of the time, she swooped in when prospective buyers came through the door and rarely bothered to introduce him unless they had financing questions. Then she made it sound as if working up numbers were his only function. She'd flash him a killer smile and prettily beg him to help the buyers with their money questions. She'd then make sure she thrust her card in their hands before they walked out the door.

She let Gavin do all the follow-up work but often cut him out during closings. Sometimes she told him the wrong time or place, or she'd "forget" to tell him when plans changed. Other times she recorded the details on the sales sheet, with only her name. He'd have to squeeze his name into the tiny space as an afterthought.

Because they quickly became one of the top-sellers in the office, Gavin kept quiet. Gavin was passing the boss's office and overheard Tammy saying that, although Gavin had closed a few deals, she'd asked those clients to work with him, so his numbers didn't suck. Outraged, Gavin stopped where they couldn't see him to listen to the rest of the conversation. Tammy went on to say she'd probably do better paired with a stronger seller, but she'd prefer to keep working with Gavin because she enjoyed a challenge and she thought she could help him with his technique. She added that he was good with numbers, so he was an asset to the team. Then she bragged about all she'd done to close the sales, even claiming credit for many of Gavin's accomplishments.

Fuming, Gavin stormed down the hall to his desk. When Tammy returned, he asked her to go with him to look at a new listing. He wasn't about to blast her in the office where others could hear. As soon as they got in the car, all his pent-up resentment spilled out. He emphasized that he was done letting her take charge of everything. He didn't mind doing the math and letting her make all the calls, but in everything else, they'd be equal partners, sharing the sales, the leads, and the credit.

Tammy's wide-eyed innocence disappeared, and in a nasty voice she said, "This partnership is over."

Shaken by the encounter, Gavin went home for the day, which turned out to be a mistake. The following morning he discovered she'd told everyone in the office Gavin had tried to force himself on her and had gotten furious when she rejected him. One of the woman agents took Gavin aside and told him she didn't believe Tammy's story, but Tammy had come back to the office, hair and suit slightly mussed, with tear filled eyes, and declared she couldn't work with Gavin ever again. Because of the situation and her stellar record, their boss had agreed to let her work alone. Many of his colleagues gave him the cold shoulder because they believed Tammy's story. Although he protested his innocence, Gavin was written up for sexual harassment and warned that another incident would cost him his job.

Gavin determined to beat Tammy's sales record this quarter to prove he'd done his share. In his quiet way, he'd built up trust with many of their clients, who often called him with questions. Also, his father had a lot of connections and sent business Gavin's way. Older couples gravitated toward him, and so did women who found Tammy's flirting with their husbands off-putting. In fact, many of the wealthier clients preferred his more refined manner.

He should not have been surprised by Tammy's dirty tricks, but she blindsided him. First, she sent out ads calling herself the top sales agent for the region, and in the office, she boasted that she'd carried Gavin.

Next, she contacted all his listings, indicating that she was taking over for him. She went out and replaced his signs with hers. She called his clients, saying she was from the agency and checking to be sure Gavin was doing a satisfactory job. During the conversation, she found out what the buyers were looking for and then sent them emails or flyers of houses that might suit their needs, particularly her listings.

Gavin had an important listing; a religious organization was selling hundreds of acres of property that had once been a campground as well as their huge office building. They planned to buy a much larger facility. Tammy called on the group to discuss some potential properties. They'd met her with Gavin, so they didn't think it was unusual for one member of the team to contact them. Knowing the group was very conservative; Tammy tearfully told her story about Gavin attacking her. The religious leaders were horrified and immediately contacted the office to say that they planned to work with Tammy rather than Gavin.

Gavin had no idea why his client had suddenly turned on him. Other prospective buyers, he contacted told him they'd already bought homes. He didn't understand what was happening until he started seeing Tammy's name next to the sales. He made sure to warn new clients about her. When people stopped falling for those tricks, Tammy resorted to cyberattacks.

In the Know

Gavin had a good following on his social network and on the online business rating sites he always received five stars. It was always nothing but positive.

Soon, however, one or two posts daily popped up written by an anonymous poster, using the screen name "In the Know." This poster claimed Gavin had cheated him.

Other posts said that Gavin was an imposter that he was trying to take credit for someone else's sales, or that Tammy Goldstone who did all the work to make him top salesman of the year. Most of the posts ended with a line, "If you want the real deal, contact Tammy Goldstone." Then it gave her contact information. The posts that hurt sales the most, though, were ones that asked: "Wonder why your mortgage rate is higher than your neighbors who bought at the same time?" They connected Gavin's name with his father's mortgage business and made it sound as if he were taking kickbacks. Or those that called him "the Italian Stallion," indicating that he'd sexually harassed women. They ended with; "Don't spend time alone with this dangerous man. He might attack you too." Facebook, Yelp, BBB, and online real estate sites became flooded with messages like these. It began to hurt Gavin's business.

At first, Gavin ignored it, hoping it would die down. Instead, the attacks only grew more vicious, and he had no way to prove Tammy was behind it.

Gavin's Solution

Gavin had recently read an article in a real estate publication about cyber-safety, that I had written. He contacted me, and soon we had a plan worked out to combat Tammy's underhanded tactics.

As I pointed out, anyone could post slams like these. It could be a rejected lover, a disgruntled former client who'd lost his house to foreclosure, someone who'd lost a bid on a house. People often read postings like this and believe them. Others jump in and side with the negative comments without any evidence, or bring up complaints that may have nothing to do with the victim's professionalism or abilities.

I outlined this information for Gavin's clients using some similar examples from other businesses. I suggested that, before passing judgment, it's important to research the facts. Check a realtor's license to see if he's received discipline for any reason, check with the Better Business Bureau, look at his references. Also, contact his former clients. When people took the time find out the truth, it quickly became clear that "In the Know" had an ulterior motive rather than a legit claim.

Soon Gavin's former clients, along with new clients who had researched his background, began posting rebuttals of "In the Know's" claims. Some of Gavin's colleagues who were aware of what was going on also posted information about his trustworthiness, his sales, and his awards.

Soon "In The Know" became the last person prospective clients would trust. Gavin also stepped up his marketing campaigns and went to more networking events. The more people got to know him, the more they learned he could be trusted. After Gavin stepped out bigger and proved he wouldn't back down or be intimidated, the attacks gradually stopped. Over time, Gavin proved himself a trusted authority in real estate and went on to become a top sales person at the brokerage. Tammy took a position at a different agency and often vied with him for regional awards, but he no longer dealt with comments from "In the Know."

Final Quick Tips

- **Keep records** of all your work and accomplishments, so you have proof of what you've done.

- **Maintain duplicate files** and find ways to get others to check
  your work and records, so you have witnesses if you need them.

- **Be vigilant about monitoring** all social media, online postings, and set up Google Alerts. Keep a close eye on their activity.

- **Pay attention to changes** in client or co-worker behaviors. The sooner you are proactive, the better. It's much easier to get a potential problem stopped immediately than to try to repair the damage after the fact.

- **Contact a lawyer. Depen**ding on the situation, if you are suffering a financial loss because of the postings of a cyberabuser like "In The Know," find out what your legal options are. There are instances where the postings if proved false have been taken down by the social sites, and ultimately you may be entitled to compensation.

CHAPTER 18

Morgan's Story

Morgan and David were both interns at a marketing firm. David had been at the company for almost six months and always outdid all the other interns by working harder and taking on extra tasks. He hoped to be offered a full-time position when he graduated.

Within a few weeks of his arrival, Morgan's work had gained so much notice that senior partners let him work on several high-profile projects. He also received praise from a major client for negotiating a deal that netted them huge TV and radio exposure, yet was well within their allotted budget.

David was seething. He'd been there longer, but the only projects he'd been allowed to work on was follow-up phone calls and emails, filling out reports, keeping track of expenses, and checking SEO to find the best angles for online advertising. None of the other interns had the opportunity to work directly with clients or show off their negotiating skills. The closest David had gotten to client meetings was when he attended one to take notes for someone who was ill.

David worried Morgan would get the full-time position, and he determined to secure his future. He posted a personal ad on Craigslist, using Morgan's name and contact information, indicating that Morgan was looking for a good time, couples welcome. People showed up at Morgan's apartment and workplace. Lewd texts arrived on

Morgan's company phone and, using a false name, David emailed copies of the ad to the partners and clients Morgan worked with, along with attachments labeled for "Morgan's eyes only."

One of the clients was a conservative company that prided itself on offering G-rated, family-friendly games and entertainment. When the head of the firm received the email, he threatened to pull his business unless the removed Morgan from the team.

Before they could fire him, a humiliated Morgan quit the internship, dropped out of school, gave up his apartment, and became a recluse. He stayed sequestered in a bedroom at his parent's house, eating and playing video games, too ashamed to show his face in public. By the time he discovered me and SIA, Morgan had gained fifty pounds and given up on life.

Morgan's Solution

Although not everyone will react so drastically to such a cyber-attack, David had chosen his revenge well. The cyberpredator had a great deal of information about Morgan's private life. He knew that Morgan was the son of a minister, had graduated from a conservative Christian high school, and had extremely strict views about sexuality, which made him shy and awkward around women. When Morgan quit the firm, David went on to secure the full-time position he desired. As the months passed with no challenge from Morgan, David grew cockier and gloated at how well his tactic had worked.

Meanwhile, Morgan's parents, concerned about their son's depression, insisted he must get a job. Too embarrassed to go out of the house, Morgan found an online job. While working online, he stumbled across the SIA website and contacted me.

Getting Help

This case was difficult because Morgan hadn't documented the ads or emails. The experienced cyber investigators employed on Morgan's behalf were able to find records of the ads online.

Letters on Morgan's behalf, explaining the case, and requesting deletion of the ads, were sent out by a reputable lawyer that Morgan's parents were willing to pay.

Although he was on his way to a successful resolution of his cyber-attacking case, Morgan badly needed counseling and emotional support to reclaim his life.

He began therapy. When he felt more comfortable going out in public, he joined a victim support group. Although many people in the group had been through much worse traumas, Morgan found that they all shared many of the same symptoms, which the group leader said was common for PTSD.

Reclaiming His Life

When Morgan was emotionally strong enough, he sent the documentation the lawyer had collected to his former employer. They had no open positions at that time but urged him to reapply for an internship in the fall, when they'd guarantee him a place. Morgan was excited, except he hadn't told them about dropping out of school.

With jobs so scarce, competition for internships and jobs can be fierce. Attacks can come in many different forms, and from any source.

CHAPTER 19

Jacob's Story

Two law students, Jacob and Marc, sat next to each other and chatted while filling out paperwork for an internship. Marc seemed quite friendly and inquired about Jacob's law school and experience. He seemed surprised that Jacob had already done a summer internship with a prestigious firm and questioned Jacob about what he'd done there. As Jacob recounted his experience, Marc nodded and said it sounded as if Jacob would be perfect for this internship.

Jacob hoped so. An internship at this prestigious firm would look wonderful on his resume, and the position was in the exact area he wanted to specialize. In questioning his chatty neighbor about his experience, Jacob discovered that Marc had a lower GPA and much less experience. Jacob hoped that meant he was a top contender for the internship.

Shocking News

A few weeks later, he was shocked to learn that Marc had gotten the position. He couldn't figure out how he'd been passed over for the internship in favor of Marc. That is until he took a break from his intense studying and logged into Tumblr. Jacob had been so busy studying for exams; he hadn't had time to check his social media accounts. He was horrified to see his name come up with defamatory posts against women and various ethnic groups. He scrolled back through the tweets and posts to find similar messages on his other social media accounts.

Jacob was sick. During the background screening, the law firm would have seen these and decided he wasn't a suitable candidate. Jacob had no proof, but he guessed Marc had planted this information to be sure Jacob, his top rival for the job, lost the position.

Jacob's Solution

The first thing I had him do was change all his passwords. Though warned against it, Jacob had used the same password for all his accounts, an easy-to-guess combination of his initials and birth date. This time he entered different passwords for each, using a random combination of letters, numbers, and symbols to make it harder for someone to guess.

Usually the next step is to document the posts and delete them immediately, but in this case, I wanted the law firm to see that these posts were written in a different style and contained content that did not match Jacob's previous posts or philosophy. Even more telling were the dates of the posts: they began the day after Jacob had filled out his application and ended the day Marc learned that he had been chosen for the internship. Once the law firm had reviewed the posts and Jacob had documented them, he deleted them.

The internal tech department at the law firm treated this situation as a security breach that could potentially cost the firm money if not detected and combated. Confidential client files, financial information, and more were kept stored on their servers. The IT team was uncertain whether Marc had hacked into their files, but if he'd done it once, he could do it again.

Meanwhile, the human resources department at the law firm did their investigation because something similar had happened to another top candidate for the internship. Only, in this case, the woman had gay-bashing tweets and posts she'd claimed she hadn't written. After both sets of posts had been traced back to Marc, the law firm terminated him and awarded the internship to Jacob, who had been their top choice until they'd seen his posts.

Marc admitted his guilt, explaining that he'd gotten friendly with each of the candidates and questioned them to see if they'd be strong competition. Only Jacob and Brooke had more outstanding qualifications than he did, so he targeted them. He watched as they filled out their applications, then he surreptitiously jotted their information and emails in a small notebook he carried. Later he used that information to hack into their accounts. Jacob's was the easiest because he had the same password for all his accounts, his initials, and birth date.

Final Quick Tips

• **SAFEGUARD PASSWORDS** By using different passwords for each account; never using special dates, names, or initials. Use a combination of letters, numbers, and symbols that aren't easy to guess, and do not store passwords online. If you worry that you won't remember all your passwords, try an online service. Be sure you create a very difficult password for that site.

• **Set up a GOOGLE ALERT** for your name. You'll receive notices of new posts by and about you.

• **CHECK YOUR NAME and variations** of your name to see what comes up. If someone with the same name has a shady reputation, try varying your name by using a middle name, a maiden name, or an initial to distinguish your posts. Be sure to let potential employers (or others who will be searching your name) know to use the full name you've chosen when looking for you online.

• **GUARD YOUR ID:** When filling out applications in public places, such as doctor's offices or schools, or at prospective places of employment, always shield your information from the view of others around you or, better yet, sit in a secluded place. Turn school IDs or driver's licenses face down if others surround you.

CHAPTER 20

Amber's Story

Amber had dreamed of being an artist from the time she was a young girl. Soon after she'd transitioned from crayons to paint brushes, her father left them, leaving her mom a broken woman. Money was tight, so Amber learned not to ask for the frivolous art supplies she desired. When she was old enough to babysit, she helped her mother with household expenses, but always set a tiny bit aside from each job and saved for paints and paper. Any spare time she had, she spent painting.

Her mother discouraged Amber's dreaminess and artistic bent, telling her to get a practical degree so she could support herself. At her mother's urging, Amber signed up for computer programming classes at the local community college. She hated every minute of it, but her mom insisted it was one of the fastest growing professions. Always a people-pleaser, Amber did what her mother wanted. She worked full time as a waitress and put herself through her first year of college.

That summer, her mom developed cancer and was gone in a matter of months. Dazed and grieving, Amber started her second semester. She had a hard time concentrating on her studies, so she spent time wandering through the school's art gallery, whenever she had time off from waitressing. The art spoke to her soul. Then, although it made her feel guilty, Amber did something very daring: she switched her major to art.

In the studio, she poured out her heartache on canvas. In spite of her sorrow, Amber was more content than she'd ever been. And when one of her paintings won first place in the school show, she was thrilled. It was the best night of her life. Not only because of the award but because she met Cat.

Cat bought Amber's prizewinning painting, and the two of them went out for coffee after the show and talked for hours. They had much in common and became fast friends immediately. They both liked weightlifting, so they met at the gym the next morning to work out. Cat ran every evening and convinced Amber to join her. Soon they were spending all their free time together.

Cat was two years older and was attending the police academy training on campus. She had an apartment a few blocks away that she invited Amber to share. It was heart-wrenching for Amber to give up the apartment she'd shared with her mother, but Cat pointed out the benefits, including saving money on rent and spending more time together. The move would mean more money for art supplies. Amber was still a bit hesitant, but with Cat's prodding, she made a move to Cat's place.

Initially, Amber moved into the second bedroom, but one night as they were watching a movie together, Cat slid closer and put her arm around Amber. Although Amber was a bit surprised, she didn't mind. Soon their relationship had progressed to the point where Cat suggested they turn the second bedroom into an art studio, and Amber readily agreed.

With that change in their relationship though, Cat became more controlling. She demanded more of Amber's time and stopped asking Amber's opinion on what movie to watch or where to meet. Cat just announced what they'd do and expected Amber to comply. It bothered Amber, but her mom had been bossy, so she gave in to keep the peace. Most of the time she didn't mind until Cat started cutting into her art time. Soon Amber couldn't paint if Cat was home. Cat insisted on spending all their time together.

The constant criticism hurt more. Before this, when the two went running, Cat was considerate of Amber's slowness. Cat would do speed bursts and then come back and jog with Amber. Now she yelled at Amber to keep up, calling her fat and lazy when she couldn't. During weightlifting, Cat jeered at Amber's technique and mocked her for being a wimp. When they played video games, Cat wasn't content to beat Amber, she tried to kill her and then gloated over her victories. Amber tried to shrug it off. She knew Cat was under a lot of pressure at the academy and had been taking quite a bit of razzing from the guys. Amber hoped it was a passing phase and would soon get better. Instead, it got worse. Cat criticized Amber's cooking and cleaning, raged about her waitressing hours, and sneered at her paintings. Amber tried harder to accommodate Cat and hid her hurt feelings.

The situation escalated the night Amber had to finish her final painting for the semester, worth one-third of her grade. She begged Cat to spend some of their time together in the studio. Cat grumbled, but she sat in the studio and kept up a running commentary, making it difficult for Amber to concentrate. Amber was working on a tricky part when Cat asked her a question. Amber didn't answer. Instead, she angled her brush to add a small detail. The next thing she knew, Cat bumped her arm, making a huge slash right through the painting.

When Amber turned to her, shocked and speechless, Cat said through clenched teeth, "Next time I ask you something, answer me." Then she added, "It doesn't matter, the painting looked awful anyway." She stormed out, leaving Amber in tears.

Amber locked the studio door and stayed up all night trying to repair the damage. She ended up with the muddied colors in the center of the painting. She was ashamed to turn it in and knew she deserved the low grade she got. What hurt more than the grade was that Cat had destroyed something that meant the world to Amber.

Then came the night Cat pulled a gun on Amber. "I could shoot you right now for practice." She said it in a joking manner, but after what had happened with the painting, Amber wasn't sure she could trust her.

After Cat had holstered her gun, Amber said that if Cat ever pointed the gun at her again, they were through. Cat whipped out the gun and said, "You mean like this." She aimed at Amber's heart. Amber tried to tell herself Cat had been drinking, but what if she joked around and pulled the trigger. Amber hoped the gun wasn't loaded, but she didn't want to take a chance.

The next morning after Cat had left for the Academy, Amber skipped class and loaded her car with everything she could fit. She had no idea where she'd go, but she headed into town to the restaurant where she worked. She asked there if anyone knew of a place she could rent. The restaurant owner offered her the guest bedroom in her house temporarily while Amber looked for an apartment. With knowing eyes, she suggested Amber unload her painting supplies in the garage.

Amber stayed there the rest of the day and ignored Cat's texts and emails. After the twentieth text demanding to know where she was, Amber blocked Cat's number. The next morning she went to class late to be sure she wouldn't run into Cat. At lunch time, she stayed in the painting studio.

Suddenly, the doors banged open, and Cat stormed in. "Nobody leaves me. Don't think you're going to get away with this." After screaming threats and obscenities, she stomped out, vowing to make Amber's life miserable. And she did.

She showed up at the restaurant during Amber's shifts, demanding to be waited on and loudly criticizing the service, "accidentally" spilling food or drink on Amber, leaving huge messes behind and no tip. She stalked into Amber's classes and caused uproars. She entered the painting studio and harangued Amber. When Amber found an apartment of her own, Cat used her police contacts to find out the address.

Then she came and banged on the door at all hours of the night until the neighbors threatened to have Amber evicted. Cat alternated between fits of rage and lame apologies. She sent emails begging Amber to come back, posted notes on her door, left roses in her car, and sent a singing telegram with a bouquet of flowers to her classroom. She continually called, texted, and emailed all Amber's classmates and coworkers, asking them to pass on her words of love.

When that wasn't effective, she returned to cruelty. The day of midterms, Amber came out to find all four of her tires slashed. A neighbor kindly gave her a ride to campus, but Amber was so shaken, she did poorly on her exams. She went to the art studio to find her latest canvas splattered with red paint. She almost collapsed in tears. She couldn't go on without help.

Amber's Solution

Amber asked several classmates for advice, and one recommended a domestic violence organization. She was refused help because her case involved a police officer. Officer involved domestic violence is particularly difficult because victims have no resources to turn too. Funded domestic violence victim resource centers won't provide assistance because they don't want to risk their relationships with law enforcement being "tainted" by aiding abuse victims. I find this repulsive. I was refused shelter by a domestic violence shelter, because of my batterer's occupation, so I understood the ramifications of being denied help. Worse yet, the officer involved domestic violence and stalking cases get classified as **"high-risk"** meaning high-risk for homicide. Therefore, a big part of the focus of Survivors in Action and the work I do was in homicide prevention and working these high-risk cases.

Amber learned about **Survivors in Action** and the OIDV (Officer Involved Domestic Violence) program that we had, and she reached out for help. I have worked many cases like Amber's, as well as with the families who have lost loved ones to stalking and domestic violence homicide. Their support of my work has inspired me to keep fighting as an advocate for all victims. All abuse victims, regardless of the predator occupation deserve the same support and should not have to live or work in fear!

The first option we had been discussing was Amber getting a restraining order. Because Cat was in law enforcement, she could potentially lose her gun and her badge.

Although that seemed like a good option, I explained that officer-involved cases tend to be high-risk, meaning Amber might end up a homicide victim. In this case, I advised against getting a restraining order. Knowing Cat's vengeful personality, Amber agreed it could be lethal, especially if Cat lost her future career in law enforcement.

Then I had Amber contact her cell phone carrier and order Cat's number blocked. She then purchased several prepaid cell phones, implementing "the bat phone" technique to use for making and receiving calls for privacy purposes. Amber spoke with her carrier's fraud/security department to report the situation and restrict access to her cell account, so it couldn't be used as a weapon to stalk her.

Next, I accompanied Amber to meet with key people in her life. We started with the art department. After I had explained to the head of the department how dangerous a jilted lover could be, the professor agreed to lock the studio whenever an intern couldn't monitor it. Students who were accustomed to coming and going at all hours of the day and night were annoyed at the new policies. Many blamed Amber. Most of her classmates were already avoiding her because they were sick of being involved in her messy breakup.

I explained to them what was happening and gave them instructions on blocking calls, texts, and emails, which the majority had already done. The professor also requested that, if asked, they refrain from divulging Amber's whereabouts. A few rolled their eyes, but most were sympathetic once they understood the situation. Some of those who were reluctant to help, changed their minds when I pointed out that, in refusing to help a victim, they were aiding the predator and placing Amber's life in danger.

I also asked everyone to send a strongly worded message to Cat saying that they didn't want to receive any more calls, texts, or emails from her, and then be sure her number is blocked. Amber also talked to mutual friends of hers and Cat's, explaining that they had broken up and asked them to please not forward any messages to Amber from her.

With the cooperation of the restaurant owner, they worked out new hours for Amber and came up with a plan of action for when Cat entered the restaurant. The hostesses were warned not to seat Cat in Amber's section even if she protested. While Cat was in the restaurant, the owner volunteered to work Amber's tables and let Amber help out in the kitchen. They only needed to use the strategy three times before Cat stopped coming in. It wasn't worth her time and money if her quarry disappeared into the kitchen the minute she arrived.

Amber's biggest worry, besides possible car sabotage, was the apartment. Cat had come to Amber's apartment drunk, the previous Saturday night and threatened to shoot her way into the apartment. She hadn't pulled a gun, but Amber worried that at some time Cat might do it.

I suggested getting a security system, but Amber had spent all her savings on new car tires. I helped her find donated security cameras for her apartment and dash cam for her car.
When Cat drove up the following Saturday night and started up the walk, she spotted the cameras and quickly retreated.

Temporary Security Measures

If you're facing an emergency situation and have no funds or are waiting for a security company to install a device, fake devices can sometimes deter stalkers. They can be purchased very inexpensively and may help to keep you safe.

Another no cost method is for the victim to take a small piece of paper and write a message that looks as if it were from the police or a security company, saying that they'd received the call and wanted her to know they had her property under 24-hour surveillance. In another situation, a victim posted a note that said: "Got the film and am reviewing it now for identification." Her stalker bolted and never returned. While it may not work for the more determined stalkers, many don't want to get caught. They want the revenge, but not the consequences.

Think creatively. Use the materials you have on hand and your knowledge of your stalker. None of these measures is a guarantee against a determined stalker, but these creative no cost methods may buy you some time and ward off an attacker temporarily until you can protect your home or apartment properly.

Additional Strategies

The situation with Cat had left Amber tense and fearful. She jumped at the slightest noise and had trouble sleeping. As she walked through town and on campus, she kept glancing over her shoulder, watching, worried, always on edge. The slightest problem or frustration had her in tears. She mentally berated herself for getting involved with Cat, and she also doubted her judgment about people, so she went into her shell and stopped talking to people. Concerned that she might be having a breakdown, she discussed her reactions with me. I assured her it was a normal reaction. Many people experience similar symptoms or have PTSD following cyberattacks or stalking. I suggested Amber go for counseling.

The mental health clinic on campus provided free services, and Amber took advantage of it. Because of her interest in art, the counselor suggested art therapy, which also helped her get over her grief, both at the loss of the relationship and her mother's death. It also decreased her anxiety and stress.

At my recommendation, Amber asked to have all her sessions kept off the record so there was no chance Cat could access them. There are great risks and a history of cyberpredators and stalkers gaining access to victim's mental health and therapy sessions and using this information against them. Be mindful of this and do what you need to do to protect yourself!

To replace the running she'd done with Cat, Amber tried yoga and found it calming. At first, she feared she'd run into Cat and always took a different and convoluted route to the on-campus studio every time. After a few weeks of not sighting Cat, Amber relaxed. She never stopped being vigilant as she walked across campus, though. When the yoga teacher mentioned retreats she was leading; Amber attended one. Knowing she wouldn't run into Cat at this secluded mountain cabin allowed Amber to relax totally in mind, body, and spirit for the first time since the breakup. She saved money so she could afford the quarterly retreats. They helped restore her equilibrium and let her breathe deeply and freely, something she rarely did in town or on campus

CHAPTER 21

Other Cases

Adam's Story

Adam grew up dirt poor in a home with an abusive, alcoholic mom. His deadbeat dad, who had been arrested multiple times for petty theft and assault, rarely paid child support. At age sixteen, while attending an alternative high school, Adam got a full-time job, intending to seek emancipation.

He had worked part-time at a neighborhood grocery store for two years as a bagger and proved himself reliable and willing to work hard. The owner hadn't bothered with a background check for the full-time job because Adam had been a model employee and was willing to work evenings, weekends, and holidays. The grocery store pay wasn't quite enough to cover monthly expenses for an apartment, utilities, and food plus car payments, so Adam applied for a job cleaning office buildings two evenings a week. Because janitorial employees had access to empty buildings, he needed both state and criminal records checks along with a credit check. His goth look and nose and eyebrow rings might make him appear scary, but Adam was happy to comply. Although he had was sent to the alternative school for truancy, he'd stayed out of trouble with the law.

When the records came back, they showed outstanding arrest warrants from several states, three civil judgments against him, and many credit cards in arrears. Adam was shocked. That was impossible. He'd never been out of the state and never borrowed money. They must have made a mistake. He double checked the reports, and all three had his social security number, full name, and birth date. The janitorial company refused to hire him.

Adam was afraid to go to the police thinking they might arrest him for the warrants. He hurried to the grocery store, hoping the owner would vouch for him. He pulled up the work schedules for the past year, and on three of the five arrest dates, Adam had been working. The owner shook his head and said it must be identity theft. Someone was impersonating Adam, but he had no idea how could he find out who it was or manage to stop them.

Adam's Solution

Adam was surprised to find an email saying that I was connecting him with a volunteer in his city, one who happened to be a private investigator. SIA volunteers helped him seek emancipation.

It took almost two years to get the issues resolved. The investigator first had to track down the person who'd stolen Adam's identity. Whenever they started closing in on the suspect, the illegal activity would cease, only to start up later in another city or state. Each time, the pattern was the same: the criminal opened bank accounts in Adam's name with a small amount of money, wrote bad checks, and then after getting arrested for illegal gambling, assault, and battery, or drunken driving, he fled to another town.

Meanwhile, because the credit bureau had Adam's new address, bill collectors came after him. His phone rang day and night with demands for money. Process servers showed up at his door. When Adam tried to explain it wasn't him, the process servers would say, "Yeah, right, kid. That's what they all say. You've been served."

Letters and notices arrived from police departments, banks, collection agencies, and from the government for tax evasion. The investigator helped Adam file police reports and sent notarized statements to all the credit bureaus and data- furnishing companies explaining the identity theft, but the warrants and bills continued to pile up.

On one of Adam's rare days off, he drove to the beach. As he headed home, the police pulled him over for burned-out tail lights. Because she discovered a warrant in his name, the officer arrested him and had his vehicle towed. No one believed his protests until the investigator arrived to bail him out.

What should have been the happiest time in Adam's life, it is not what he experienced. He'd had obtained emancipation, he'd graduated from high school, and the grocery store owner was letting him work overtime hours. Betty had gotten him a part- time job with a landscaping company, and he loved that work so much, he planned to start his own business. For the first time in his life, he ate three meals every day, he'd made enough money to buy a beat-up car, and he even had a computer and stacks of computer games. All his dreams had come true, except one... clearing his name.

A break in the case came when the identity thief managed to get a driver's license in rural Louisiana. A detective in that state followed up on the lead and captured the criminal. Finally, they had their man, a man who turned out to be Adam's father.

Once his father had been arrested and charged with identity theft along with all his other crimes, Adam and the investigator went to work, clearing his name. Now they had the proof they needed to back up their claims. Through the police in Louisiana, they also discovered the reasons behind the identity theft.

After his parents had divorced, his father had taken Adam's social security card and used it to avoid paying child support and taxes. But as his gambling addiction and drinking increased, the warrants for his arrest piled up. He began his nomadic lifestyle, moving to new cities to stay one step ahead of the law and his creditors. When he was flush, he lived well. But more often, he was broke. He'd either steal what he needed or use Adam's name to open a bank account and write bad checks.

Adam's father had been abusing Adam's identity long before Adam discovered it. His father had accumulated so many debts and warrants that it complicated the case. Eventually, the investigator succeeded in getting Adam a clean criminal record.

However, the story didn't end there. Adam's case was one of many where teens get deprived of their identities. Unfortunately, parents who steal their children's identities happen quite commonly. Parents use children's names to avoid taxes, alimony, or child support. In other cases, parents collect death benefits for their child. Because these victims were reported dead on paper, as teens or adults, they could not open bank accounts, get credit, or collect tax refunds, if they were working.

Like Adam, many discovered crimes had been committed in their names. Teens are not the only ones who face identity theft.
I have worked with victims, many of whom have also experienced cyberstalking, to find attorneys through NACA (National Association of Consumer Advocates.) The lawyers in this network will take identity theft cases on contingency. In some cases, data brokers and credit agencies get sued, and the victims won large settlements.

Clearing Up Credit

Because Adam had filed police reports and had sent a notarized affidavit of forgery to the credit bureaus and collection agencies, the creditors and banks should not have been pursuing him for debts that he did not owe. Two collection agencies, in particular, had violated state and federal credit-collection laws by threatening him on the phone. One had even threatened that they knew where he lived and his deadbeat ass was going to get a beating if he didn't pay. Adam utilized the NACA network, and an attorney took his case on contingency. The attorney sued the data broker, which had continued to furnish his information to creditors despite the affidavit, as well as the collection agencies that had used illegal methods to harass him. Adam won a settlement, and that helped him completely restore his credit.

Additional Self-Help Action Steps:

Reestablishing an identity can be a long, time-consuming process as Adam learned. It can often be difficult to prove your identity to the authorities' or creditors' satisfaction. Here are several precautionary steps to follow after your credit gets cleared:

•   Request the credit bureaus put a **Fraud Alert** on your credit profiles.

•   Add a **Consumer Statement** to all credit bureau records that states: My name is X, and accounts have been opened without my permission using my social security number. Do not open accounts without first contacting this consumer at the following phone number: XXX-XXX-XXXX.

•   **Monitor credit reports** every six months to be sure to check that no old or inaccurate information gets included. Even after successful lawsuits against credit bureaus and collection agencies, one or two accounts could reappear. Past information often gets inadvertently added when accounts are researched and updated. If these companies continue to give out incorrect information after you've notified them of the situation, contact an attorney.

Final Quick Tips

•   Be wary. People can create any identity they choose online. Safeguard your private information and use screen names that don't give away your real identity or location.

•   Be patient and persistent. If you've been a victim of identity theft, or financial fraud, recovery takes time.

•   Consult an attorney. Consult an attorney that represents clients that have experienced identity theft, debt collector abuse, and inaccurate credit reporting. Most take these cases on contingency.

CHAPTER 22

Inside a CyberStalker's Mind

I have had the opportunity over the years to interact with stalkers and cyberstalkers to gain insight from their perspective which in turn has helped me become more effective in aiding victims.

One cyberstalker was sorry for his actions and wished to make amends for what he'd done. As part of his sentencing requirements, he'd been forbidden to contact his victims, but he wanted to apologize to those he'd hurt. He offered to help support my work aiding victims of cyberabuse and share his experiences in the hopes that they might help other victims. (Note: All names, including that of the cyberstalker, have been changed to protect identities.)

Martin's case is bit unusual as he was a serial cyberstalker. Other than sexual predators, cyberstalkers typically target one person: someone they feel has wronged them, someone they need to surpass or control, or someone with whom they long to have a relationship. Martin, though, went after multiple victims, some he knew and some he didn't.

Martin's Story

Martin grew up in a small town in the UK, the oldest of three children. Both of his parents were janitors and insisted the family attend church on Sunday mornings. Although the children fought, especially Martin and his younger brother, they got along well.

Bullied and shy, Martin admitted to being bullied at school. He mainly endured name calling, but one student demanded Martin lunch money almost every day for a whole year. Later after Martin launched a social media account where people could ask him questions, anonymous visitors posted nasty questions. During his school years, he felt like an outsider. By secondary school, he was labeled as a "geek." When he was younger, Martin had a crush on a girl but was too shy to approach her. He'd get nervous around her and only watched her from afar. That pattern was repeated later in adult life as he developed crushes on other girls. But the Internet, which he started using in his early twenties, made it easier for him to contact people who caught his interest.

First Victims

Ann happened to be one of those people. He followed her on social media, avidly watching her every post, snooping to see what she was doing by "friending" her friends. He checked to see who she talked to and then went to their pages to find out more about her friends. If their profiles were private, he sent friend requests so that he could keep tabs on Ann's interactions with them.

He looked up any males she contacted, trying to figure out if she had a relationship with them.

When Ann talked to other people, Martin bombarded her with texts to find out why. Perhaps to scare off male competition, he set up a fake Facebook page, pretending to be Ann and came out to one of her lesbian friends. For about five years, he obsessed over and harassed Ann.

Then he switched his attention to Trisha. Martin tried to control his obsession this time and managed to reduce his daily checks of Trisha's accounts to under ten. With Ann, it had been between twenty and thirty per day. He didn't take Trisha's rejection well either.

Uncontrollable Rage

Most of the women he'd targeted were members of the same forum, all of them were fans of a pop group. Whenever anyone unfriended or unfollowed him, Martin went ballistic. He felt rejected and attacked them, setting up another account to send abusive and obscene messages, often after getting drunk. Soon more and more people started blocking or deleting him.

When he confronted one girl about blocking him, she called him a "perv." He tried to convince her differently, but after several messages back and forth, she refused to change her mind. She, too, received indecent messages.

Celebrity Stalking

Next Martin, who had been a longtime fan of the pop group and attended all their concerts, turned his attention to the lead singer, particularly after he learned she'd sympathized with the girls he'd attacked, and she'd blocked him herself. He set up a new Twitter account.

According to the rock star, Martin acted overly familiar. At first, his messages made her uncomfortable, and later they became more graphic. The sexual messages turned into a rape threat.

Martin admitted being obsessed with the star and sending inappropriate tweets, but claimed he couldn't remember making the rape threat. He didn't deny that he did it, and agreed it came from one of the pseudonyms he was using. Because he often sent abusive messages when he was drunk, it's possible that may have been the case.

Each time he was blocked, he started a new account, determined to apologize, only to end up cyber- harassing the women when he was drunk or angry. A warning messages from the pop group's online administrator and an article in the news about the pop star's cyberstalker halted Martin temporarily. But his anger built up and eventually spurred another flurry of lewd tweets.

Getting Help

At the convincing of a friend, Martin went to the local mental health clinic and was prescribed antidepressants. That helped for a while, and he stayed off social media for several weeks. But after getting drunk at a concert, he cyber-attacked a girl he liked because she'd been talking to another guy.

When the girl blocked him, Martin blamed her friend and texted a sexually explicit photo to that girl. She called and yelled at him. Martin realized how bad it had gotten, and knew he needed help to stop. He went to the local police and confessed. The officers confiscated his computer and attempted to get in touch with the victims – sixteen, in all. Of that number, six agreed to testify.

Light Sentence

Martin received a sentencing of three years of probation and one hundred hours of community service. He had to attend court-mandated drug and alcohol and a sex-offenders program. The court banned him from posting on social networks or public online forums for three years and forbid him to contact any of the victims.

Martin was relieved not to get a jail sentence, but he did say he felt his sentence was too lenient, given what he'd done. Many of the victims agreed. In an interview afterward, the lead singer admitted she lives in fear, never knowing if she would be attacked again.

With the penalties for cyberstalking being so light, Martin believes it doesn't serve as enough of a deterrent. Before he went to the police he worried about what might happen to him, so he looked up similar cases online. When he saw that the usual penalties were probation and community service, he didn't worry. He admitted, that if offenders were sentenced to time in jail, he would have ceased all activity immediately.

Moving On

The ban from social media has kept Martin from cyberstalking others for the time being, but in the future, he plans to keep in mind how much he hurt the victims and keep in mind that next time the penalties will be stiffer. He also hoped that telling his story would let his victims know that he regretted his actions. And he hopes to prevent others from falling victim to cyberstalkers.

He reiterated many of the tips found in this book and stressed online and personal safety, in particular being careful when extricating yourself from a relationship with someone who has rage management issues. While driven by fury, they are irrational and dangerous.

He also warned not to friend everyone who asks. Don't let the desire for friends or to feel popular override common sense. Check profiles before friending anyone. If they have no history of posts, don't accept their request. There's a good chance they just created that account and will use it to harass you. Re- member that online people can pretend to be whoever they want to be.

Report any inappropriate messages immediately. If enough people had reported Martin messages as abuse, the administration might have banned him from the social media sites, which may have caused him to rethink his actions sooner.

CHAPTER 23

Avoid Being a Victim

Staying safe is not only a question of following safety measures, but it's also an attitude what I call "mindset." One of the first steps to avoiding being a victim is to identify your tendency toward it. If you see yourself as a victim, others will too. Even if you find that you have a victim mindset, you can change it. Once you've accomplished that, you can better protect yourself and avoid dangerous relationships.

My first days spent in firearms training classes and self-defense classes both shared the same pattern of instruction teaching about the mindset. A mindset my instructors said, will decide your future.

Avoiding Becoming a Cyberabuse Victim

Here are self-help action steps that can prevent you from becoming a victim of cyberabuse. They may take a few hours to implement, but the payoff is protection from the hundreds of hours it takes to undo the damage of a cyberstalker.

- Don't give out personal information offline or online. Keep your home address, location, names of family members, phone number, and all other identifying information private. Teens, especially, should be wary about giving out any personal details, particularly to any friends they make online.

•   Install spyware protection and keep your settings high on your firewalls. Be sure the spyware protection is a reputable company, and be extremely careful that you download it from the company website, not a third party.

•   Visit my websites: www.consultwithalexismoore.com and www.alexismoore.com I provide recommendations for products to help you stay "Moore Secure."

•   Create a designated email account separate from your personal and business email account. Use this for online ordering, signing up for social media accounts, and registering for events. Give it as your contact email to strangers, salespeople, or acquaintances. It will help protect your account from spam, hackers, and spyware.

•   Do not fill out all the fields when registering online. If something is not required, don't provide it. Avoid filling in birth dates and locations. Also, consider entering safer addresses (e.g., business, school address or Post Office Box or Mail Receiving Station rather than your home address). If the account you are registering for has no reason to require this information and no need to contact you, you may want to fill it in with "Not Applicable" or 100
Anywhere Street, Anytown.

•   Guard your email, and social media account logins the same way you do your credit card information. All it takes is one person knowing your login and password for the rest of the world to learn it.

•   Read and monitor privacy policies. Always read the privacy policies before you sign up for a site. If they have options for sharing information, make sure you opt out of third-party sharing. Many online sites change their privacy frequently, so keep up to date on the changes.

•   Watch what you're sharing. Strangers can learn a lot about you by the places you visit, the pictures you post, and the things you enjoy.

•   Ask friends and family to be cautious. Tell them your concerns about privacy and request that they do not post information that violates your privacy. Also, give them information about protecting themselves online, so they can avoid becoming a victim as well.

•   Password protect all accounts, including all your tech devices, cell phones, emails, bank accounts, insurance, and credit cards with a secure password that would be difficult for anyone to guess. Change these at least twice a year. Do it more frequently if you've ever been hacked or been the target of cyberstalking.

•   Choose unusual answers for your security questions. Select answers that belong to someone else. Instead of using the name of the street you grew up on, use the street name of your childhood enemy. For the name of your favorite pet, substitute your neighbor's yappy dog. For favorite food, write peanut butter, if you're allergic to peanuts. Make sure they're answers you'll easily remember, but that other's, (even spouses and family members) will never guess.

•   Be suspicious of any incoming emails, telephone calls, texts, or messages that ask for your identifying information. The caller ID spoof can mimic your bank's caller ID. It is very easy for a cyberstalker posing as a banking representative, utility, credit card representative, or your cell phone provider to obtain your private information. Most institutions do not contact you to ask for this information; they already have it. Hang up and call the institution directly to be sure that you were not a target of a cyberstalker.

•	Never give out your Social Security Number unless you are sure of who is asking for it and why. With your "social," as they call it in the business, a cyberstalker now has access to every part of your life.

•	Don't open emails or click on links from strangers. Email is one of the easiest ways for people to install keylogger programs, viruses, and other malware on your computer. If messages come from someone you know, but it has a strange subject line or no subject at all, and it contains only a link, don't open it. Email your friends or relatives to ask if they sent it. If they didn't, it is possible their accounts got hacked as well.

•	Conduct an Internet search on your name (and also on your phone number) every few months. Be sure nothing damaging has posted. A cyberstalker may have created social media accounts, web pages, or blogs about you. Only you, can stay on top of how your name is used online. Always do a search like this before applying for jobs or colleges.

•	Make your real name unique online. If someone has the same name as you and they have a shady reputation or espouse views that are not your own, change your name to make it different. Add your middle initial or middle name, use your maiden name, go by a nickname or revert to your full name. Make sure everyone knows which person is you, particularly employers or others where your reputation is important. It will also prevent you from being targeted by someone who is really after another person who has the same name.

•	Sign up for Google Alerts for your name and any screen names/ pseudonyms you use online. You'll get messages when someone posts something about you.

- Check your credit reports regularly. You can request a free copy of your credit once a year directly from the three credit bureaus, Equifax, Experian and TransUnion. If you have a reason to be concerned, check them frequently. It is worth the additional cost to be sure you have not been a victim of identity theft. Go directly to each bureau; you will not damage your credit rating if you obtain a copy directly from the bureaus. Avoid paying third parties to obtain copies of the report because they usually charge more than the credit bureaus, and you'll end up on another mailing list.

- Inform your bank and credit companies that no one is allowed to make any changes to your accounts, no matter what the reason. You can have special instructions placed on your account that all changes must receive verification, by calling you first. In particular, this is an important step to take following a breakup. Even if you are reasonably certain that your former partner is trustworthy, this is a good practice for moving forward on your own.

- Use only a secure designated PC for online banking and other private transactions, if you can afford to do so. Switch to a different device for surfing the web, gaming, and accessing social media. Preventing viruses from being picked up and maintaining a more cyber-secure environment is imperative.

- Be proactive if you encounter something suspicious – a weird phone call, or text, unusual activity on an account, or a dwindling account that can't be explained by your bank. It could be a cyberstalker, so act accordingly. Change all your accounts, and close the account or, ideally, change banks. Check your credit report. Note anything else that appears strange.

- Document and report all incidents in your "Events Time Line" and create the "public safety paper trail."
- Have your PC checked by a tech professional

Have your tech equipment "inspected" once per year just like your regular yearly physical; a PC needs a "health check-up" too. If you're having problems or you think you may be a target do it more often. If you're experiencing cyberstalking incidents, it is highly possible that your computer is compromised. Have someone in the know check it for spyware and other viruses.

- If you think you have a cyberstalker, move fast. Most people don't take action because they think they're crazy or imagining things. Record incidents including time, place, and what happened, in the "Events Time Line." Victims of repeated attacks tend to become paralyzed with fear. The faster you take action and block their ability to hurt or harass you, the sooner they lose interest.

If you have a blog, website, professional profile, or business account online, follow these additional steps:

- Protect your privacy when registering your domain name. The information you use to sign up is public record and easily obtainable online. Domain proxy services offer some protection but can be pressured or forced into revealing the information. Use a business address, preferably a post office box or mail receiving station that does not reveal your home location. And set up an email that is used exclusively for managing the domain.
- Never discuss private or family business online. This rule is extremely important for professionals, especially those who are very visible.
- Use your work address for correspondence or a rent a private mailbox. Unless people need to come to your

place of business or mail items to you, never post your address online.

• Create a separate persona under a different name (e.g., nickname, maiden name) or use a pseudonym for social and public use.

• Don't post your email address. Instead, create a simple contact form where people can post and submit their information. You choose when, if or how you will respond.

• Require people to sign up for an account to post comments on your site or blog. Or activate the option to track IP addresses of those making comments. Blogs and websites usually have settings to filter spam, but they can't filter out cyberpredators who are personally targeting you. Most cyberpredators, though, will avoid sites where there is a possibility of being tracked or identified.

• Post a policy for acceptable postings. Establishing guidelines can help to eliminate negative or flaming comments.

• Set up an approval process for comments. Either you or someone you designate should read each comment before posting. Check your comments regularly and delete and block any users and material that are unacceptable.

• Use web counters or other free registry dashboard services to record all incoming traffic to your blogs and websites. Web counters allow you to identify who is viewing your site because the registry records the IP address, date, time, city, state, and Internet service provider. These records are useful for marketing, but more importantly, they provide a valuable safeguard in protecting your website or blog from being targeted by a cyberpredator.

CHAPTER 24

Thwarting a Cyberabuser

Getting out of the victim mindset and deciding to take charge of your life can be the single most empowering step you can take. Always begin by following all the Self-Help Action Steps listed to secure your personal information and help maintain your privacy.

Cyberabuse runs the gamut from simple annoyances, to bullying and harassment to cyberstalking and cybercrime, which includes financial and identity theft, as well as non-consensual pornography, even terrorism, and other violent acts. Different methods of defense are necessary for each type of attack, and every case is unique, so there is no one size fits all solution. By reading the case studies, you can find a variety of ideas for stopping cyberpredators, and you can contact me for help.

Be Creative

In addition to getting support and assistance from others, come up with creative solutions of your own. Once you get out of the victim mindset and reclaim your power, you will be amazed at how inventive you can be.

Unless the attacker is a stranger, you know quite a bit about this person and can use that knowledge to thwart him or her. Make a list of any weak points, dislikes, and fears. Also, list the ways people have stopped your attacker in the past. The goal is to figure out what would upset the cyberpredator most and use that knowledge to stop the abuse.

For example, if the attacker thrives on attention from peers, try to prevent the cyber-harassment from going viral. If the goal of the cyberabuse is to make you squirm or live in fear, work on maintaining an outer calm and poise that will frustrate their efforts. If the attacker thrives on secrecy and works in a high- profile industry, particularly one that would frown on abuse, find a way to go public with the information.

These strategies won't always work, and depending on the attacker, they may backfire and cause an increase in the abuse, or the attacker may come up with new methods.

First and foremost, keep in mind that it is imperative not to think or act like a victim. By taking proactive steps using these self-defense strategies I have shared in this book, and along with those you come up with on your own, you will find yourself in a much better position than sitting idle and doing nothing.

Do not allow the cyberpredator or stalker to take from you precious time, which you will never get back, nor your sanity and health.

CYBERBULLYING

Physical bullying usually leaves behind outward signs, but in cyberbullying those scars are internal.

The pain is often not evident until the victim makes the devastating choice to commit suicide. What kids do as a joke or to be accepted as part of the group can have awful results. If you're on the receiving end of teasing or cruelty, you know the pain, the humiliation, the shame firsthand. As an observer, you've likely thought about the pain that bullying causes. With the internet, you can't always see the results, so it's easy to go overboard with cruelty. But whether the abuse is occurring online or offline, there's one main rule: **Speak out!**

The number one issue with bullying and cyberbullying is the silence surrounding it. Kids, teens, and often adults, who experience being, bullied don't tell anyone. Their reasons range from being macho to not ratting on others. They may be ashamed of what's happening and not want anyone to know. The first and most important step is to tell someone.

Break the code of silence. The unspoken rule that you should never rat on your peers is one of the reasons cyberbullying, and bullying, in general, is so rampant. Many people see what's going on. Perhaps some even join the harassment, so they don't become targets. But the only way to stop bullying and cyberbullying is to **SPEAK OUT!**

Tell the truth, let authorities know what's happening, inform parents, school administrators, coaches, employers or anyone in charge of the group. If you're afraid of the repercussions, do it **anonymously.** Send a letter, make a call from a private phone, or go to the library and set up an email using a fake name. Not everyone will listen, but keep speaking out until someone hears and helps.

In the past, some schools or organizations didn't take bullying or cyberbullying seriously. Their attitude was "kids will be kids" or "it's all a part of growing up." Few educational systems or groups have that attitude anymore. With the increasing number of teen suicides, most have strong policies in place to prevent abuse of any kind, either online or offline. Federal policy is mandating that schools institute rules protect students from being bullied.

Additional Strategies

Following all the usual rules can be helpful, but sometimes a little creativity can bring fast results.

One teen set up an auto-response to let the bully know her messages were getting forwarded to the school principal and the bully's parents.

Here's a sample of the messages Kenley sent: "I'm unable to read or respond to your text (or email) at this time, but copies of your messages are getting forwarded to Mr. Steven Jefferson at Central High School, Ms. Mahalia Jones-Kennedy, and Mr. Rutherford Jones. They will be in touch with you." Without reading the messages, Kenley forwarded it to the appropriate parties.

In Kenley's case, the auto response proved effective. No more messages were received. If the messages hadn't worked, she could also have forwarded the texts and emails to local law enforcement, an attorney, and any other authorities the bully might fear.

After changing the privacy settings on her social media accounts, making copies of the posts, and deleting the nasty and cruel comments, Kenley also placed announcements in the header of each account that said, "Due to reports of inappropriate postings, all activity on this site is monitored. Anyone who posts derogatory or defamatory comments in violation of site policy will have their account terminated." Sometimes messages like the ones Kenley sent will enough to stop the cyberbullying. Bullies want their peers to laugh with them, but few are willing to have their texts exposed to authorities. Messages like those also have another advantage. Bullies are out for a reaction. In this case, they got no response, which was disappointing.

If someone else is bullied

•   **Speak out!** Whether it's you or someone you know who is being bullied or cyberbullied, tell someone immediately.

Let people know. Inform the authorities (school principal and administration, boss, club leader, coach, pastor at your church).

• **Don't participate.** Sometimes you know bullying is occurring, and you're pressured to join in. Taking a stand against it may be unpopular and may even make you a target too. If you're not strong enough to just say no, simply make an excuse for not joining in. Avoid the bullies for a while or find different online activities. There's no excuse for abuse.

• **Don't hit like or send**. If you see a messages or picture that will hurt someone, don't like it or pass it on. Instead, send messages to the sender, saying you don't agree.

• **Don't get caught up in arguing or judging;** just point out that it's hurtful, illegal, or against social media policy. You can word the messages so that it sounds as if you care about the bully and want to prevent him or her from getting in trouble. Also, send messages to the person being bullied to show that not everyone agrees with what's happening. Sometimes that one message of support can keep victims hanging on and stop them from harming themselves.

• **Go against the crowd**. Sometimes all it takes is for one person to say "No" or "Stop" or "Let's do something else." It's easier to go along with everyone else if they've singled out someone to bully. Everyone just follows the lead of the person who came up with the idea. Everyone wants to be part of the in the crowd rather than one of the victims, so it takes guts to step out and say, "I'm not going to participate." You may find, that others in the group agree with you and will join you. Many people become silent, but unwilling, participants out of fear. When one person has the courage to declare "Enough," others who have been afraid to speak up will follow your lead. Be the brave one, the one willing to set limits.

•   **Identify the bullies.** The goal is not to shame or punish them, but to get them help. Many bullies experience abuse at home, so they need counseling to deal with their issues. Kids who feel good about themselves have no need to bully others.

•   **Educate the group.** Ask to have speakers visit the school, workplace, or organization to talk about bullying. Invite trained experts who can emphasize the effects and consequences of cyberbullying.

•   **Get parents and other adults involved.** The more adults who take a stand against bullying and set limits on it, the less likely bullying is to happen. Parents who monitor their children's Internet and cell phone use can deter bullying and detect when their children are targets.

•   **Campaign for anti-bullying policies.** If your school, job, organization, or sports team has not set a policy for dealing with bullies, push to institute one. Make sure it includes help for the bullies, not just punishment. It should include both online and offline rules.

Dealing with Cyberabuse

Be relentless about getting the non-consensual porn, humiliating pictures or information removed; report it to the websites.

Stopping Cyberabuse

•   Take all cyberabuse seriously. It's easy to brush off early attempts as someone being in a bad mood, or perhaps it was a mistake on their part. But keep a record of any messages that are cruel, unkind, or contain threats or sexual innuendos. Later these may be needed as proof of an ongoing problem. Record these in the "Events Time Line."

• Take time to think. Don't overreact or shoot back an immediate response. Consider whether or not to answer. If you find yourself experiencing harassment on the phone, don't respond. Instead say, "Excuse me, I need to hang up now." If the harasser calls back, let it go to voice mail.

• Let others know. The natural tendency is to keep quiet about nasty messages, but the more the abuser gets away with the harassment, the more likely it is to escalate. One employee who received several emails from a colleague that were particularly nasty in tone took action by answering one email and copying their boss on her reply. She wrote: "I don't have that particular information yet, but I've copied our supervisor, so he'll know that you need those statistics as soon as they become available." Her colleague, knowing that what she said might end up being copied to their supervisor, immediately changed her tone in future emails.

• Getathird-partymonitor.Ask for help with documentation. Having a neutral party viewing and collecting the messages can help you avoid being affected by them. Another person will also be better able to judge when the tone becomes dangerous or threatening.

• Counteract the negative. If like Gavin, someone is posting defamatory messages on a site over which you have no control, ask colleagues, clients, and friends to balance the messages with positive ones. Be sure your supporters don't engage with the cyberpredator; they should ignore what was said and post only positive messages. Keep going until the positive messages outweigh the negative ones. Often this will spur others to write positive things about you as well. Sometimes seeing that you get more praise each time they criticize you will frustrate harassers enough to stop. If the complimentary posts come from a variety of people and the derogatory comments are from the same source, people reading the messages will conclude your detractor must be wrong.

CYBERSTALKING

Cyberstalkers are usually extremely vengeful and persistent. In many cases, destroying their victims is more important to them than getting caught. They're willing to risk their lives to get back at the victim. Threats of law enforcement rarely deter them; many see themselves as above the law. In many cases, they may be mentally unbalanced, which makes them especially dangerous.

Cyberstalkers fall into two categories: Those who only use the internet to keep track of and terrorize their victims, and those who also physically stalk them. In the latter case, these cyberstalkers may issue online threats as well as use electronics to help them locate their prey. If your cyberstalker is physically threatening you, following you, or intimidating you in any way, take precautions for your physical safety and use some of the strategies in the Action Steps to throw them off your trail.

Additional Tips

•   Search your name online to see what information is available. Several Internet aggregators provide detailed information about people based on their phone numbers, email addresses, and names. Viewers can see your address, an aerial picture of your house, the cost and size of your home, your place of employment, your salary range, your hobbies, your social networks, and names of family members and relatives.

Much of this information is free, but paid services called "data brokers" give even more detailed information. All of this can provide valuable clues for your stalker.

To protect you, find the company's privacy policies and get this information deleted. Spokeo is an example of one of these services. To clear your information there, go to the site, and pull up your name. Copy the URL, and then click on the Privacy link (bar along lower edge). When you click on the Opt Out button, it will ask for the URL. Check your name to see if it's associated with previous addresses. You can clear other family members' data as well. Also, do this on other aggregate sites that appeared during your search.

• Enlist witnesses. Find friends or coworkers who can back up your story. Include their information in your "Events Time Line."

Some law enforcement personnel tend to dismiss claims of cyberstalking or may not know how to deal with them. Having witnesses who corroborate your story along with a detailed log will verify that you aren't just hysterical, overwrought, or imagining things.

If the cyberstalking includes financial fraud or changes to your accounts, bills, or appointments, follow the steps listed under cybercrime. If you are also experiencing physical stalking, see the safety tips identified herein as well.

CHAPTER 25

Staying Safe in Dangerous Situations

Cyberstalkers are categorized in two ways: those who operate solely via electronic means and those who use electronics to target or track victims. Cyberabuse may escalate to physical stalking. The stalker uses phones, computers, and other electronic devices as weapons. If your situation involves cyberabuse and stalking, you'll need additional means to protect yourself. The most important steps are to stay safe and elude the stalker.

Always think about your safety at all times. Avoid poorly lit isolated areas, establish safe zones, travel in groups, install surveillance equipment, vary your daily routines, take different routes to work and appointments, carpool and ride share, learn self-defense techniques, and keep a log of all encounters with your stalker. Continue to report all incidents to law enforcement. Get a restraining order immediately, if the stalker has hurt or abused you in any way or is using tech to stalk you,

Begin with What You Know

The fact that your stalker is someone you know can be to your advantage in several ways. First of all, you know what this individual looks like; it's easy to pick him or her out of a crowd. Secondly, you know the places your stalker frequents, and you can avoid those. You may know your pursuer's work hours and schedule. All of this information can be valuable. Spend time writing down everything you can. Include the stalker's relatives and friends, their addresses, and contact information as well as the stalker's. Record his or her extracurricular activities and acquaintances, employment history and colleagues, make and model car, favorite restaurants, and activities, and any other personal details, along with a detailed description, any pictures, and credit card/bank account/social security number if known.

You also have one additional advantage. If you've dated or lived with this person, you know a lot about what motivates him or her. Add this information to the file. Often this knowledge will spur ideas for slowing or stopping the predator. It also gives you insight into character and motivation, which means being able to more easily predict the stalker's patterns, thoughts, and plans. You also know what upsets him or her, and how far this person will go. All of this can help you plan your strategy.

Collect all the information in a file or keep it online. Give a duplicate copy of this information to at least one person you trust. The police, risk management consultant, like me, or an investigator will find these records invaluable. And if something happens to you, the file will be useful for tracking the perpetrator down.

If a stranger is stalking you, find out as much about this person as you can. Hire an investigator to gather data, and keep track of any details you discover, including email addresses, phone number, and the times that the stalking occurs. If the stalker sends gifts or letters, try to track them back to the sender. Sometimes even the slightest detail can provide clues to the person's identity. Putting a face and name to the faceless entity stalking you makes it easier to protect yourself. The more you know about your stalker, the more easily you can elude him or her.

Foiling a Stalker

Stalkers are devious, so you need to be working to stay one step (or more) ahead. If the stalker frequently shows up at places you're going but doesn't seem to trail you physically, it's highly probable that the stalker has access to your tech devices including your phone and email accounts. Begin by changing all passwords. Also, try making plans with friends using a different phone (calling from work, a relative's phone, VOIP, or use "Bat Phone" technique), opening a new email account on someone else's computer or at the library and emailing from there.

Be Creative!

CHAPTER 26

My Story

When I fled from an abusive relationship, I was stalked and cyberstalked relentlessly. There were also private investigators engaged to follow me. Combining creativity, and knowledge of technology, my cyberstalker drained my bank account, shut off my utilities, cut off my insurance, turned off my phone, canceled appointments, bought things using my charge cards sinking me into debt, and harassed me at home and work.

I lost two jobs after the cyberstalker targeted my colleagues and supervisors. My friends and family avoided all contact with me after he threatened their lives. Process servers were sent to my friends and families homes some brandishing guns, pounding on their doors day and night.

Living in Fear

But nothing could compare to the terror of the phone calls describing what I was wearing and where I was standing right that minute. Repeatedly I was told that he'd have someone throw me in the trunk of a car, the car towed to the local scrap yard, my body incinerated, and nobody would know.

I knew what he was capable of; he'd almost killed me when we lived together, and several times recently, cars had attempted to run me off the road. I needed to throw this predator off my tail, but with his knowledge of all of my private information, that seemed impossible. Using my creativity, I came up with a plan to confuse my predator. I call it the Red Herring Technique.

Red Herring Technique

In mystery stories, red herrings are clues that distract or mislead readers. They cause readers to jump to false conclusions. Determined to make my life a mystery to my stalker, I employed this new technique. Knowing that my phone records, emails, and credit information were in my cyberstalker's hands, I created a "fake" life. I played tricks on him so he could never be sure he had the right information on my whereabouts. I frequently called phone numbers that had nothing to do with my real life or plans. I called doctor's offices I didn't plan to visit, hair salons I didn't use, law offices I didn't use, restaurants I never intended to frequent. I applied to rent apartments I would never live in and requested credit cards I would never use. This way, my stalker didn't know where I was all the time. He had no clue. Constantly following the "trail of flawed leads," kept him busy and frustrated... saving me time. Meanwhile, I used prepaid disposable phones to make my actual appointments.

But I was still trapped, never knowing if or when the stalker might attack. For all I knew, my stalker might get so angry he'd break into my apartment, and drag me off. Meanwhile, my life was a mess. Friendless, penniless, jobless, and depressed, I struggled through most days.

I stayed confined to my small apartment most of the time. Formerly an avid jogger, I gave up my daily runs. I was too frightened, and it was much too risky for me to attend classes. I finished my college undergraduate degrees and law school degree online. My social life was non-existent, I was gaining weight, and I was miserable.
I made stalking me difficult, but the stalker made life even harder for me. The years stretched before me, a desolate, unbearable life with no way out. I couldn't go on like this. I

even considered suicide. Then an opportunity came my way that offered me a way out, although I didn't realize it at the time.

Hiding in Plain Sight

Despondent, I sat watching TV. The grim news stories are flashing past matched my bleak mood. Then the local station aired a plea from an assemblywoman who wanted abuse survivors to support legislation she was introducing. She asked to meet with victims who were willing to speak out against domestic violence. The request seemed aimed directly at me, but for me, the hurdles were too great.

Would they care about the story of a frumpy, overweight woman scared to death to leave her apartment? Even if they did, could I travel that distance without my ex-discovering my destination? If he had any inkling of my plan, he'd put an end to it...and to me.

Although it meant putting my life at risk, I had to do this. I had to speak out, to tell the truth of what life was like for victims. Even if I couldn't help myself, perhaps I could help others. Trembling, I picked up my latest disposable phone and dialed.

A Terrifying Ride

Although I'd used the Red Herring Technique to lure the stalker in the opposite direction, I drove to the briefing, hands clenched on the wheel, petrified that any minute my ex's vehicle would appear in her rearview mirror. I didn't know my way around downtown, so I'd have trouble getting away. Vulnerable and exposed in the parking garage, I regretted coming. The only thing that kept me going was the thought that my testimony might convince lawmakers to protect victims. I also did not want to be another statistic that others could read in the newspaper. I believed that if I were going to be stalked and killed, I wanted the opportunity to be heard.

Reaching onto the seat beside me, I lifted the thick file on my stalker. I had brought my "Events Time Line." It contained all of my incident logs, police reports, and the other information I had gathered the past two years. My palms were sweaty, and my heart was pounding, I hugged the files to my chest, knowing they'd do little to stop a bullet.

Speaking Out

A brave survivor and I were the only two victims at the hearing. We told our stories at the assembly hearings, but the other woman refused to take the podium at the press conference afterward. Glancing around the room at what seemed like hundreds of news cameras, all I wanted to do was hide. My head was pounding worse than ever because of the head injury I sustained, and I truly didn't want to be in front of all of those flashing lights. Bright lights made my condition worse, but I knew I had to speak out and take back my life, or I would live in fear forever.

In a shaky, hesitant voice, I recounted my story. Afterward, one of the police officers told me, "Today is probably the luckiest day of your life. Nobody will ever forget you. All of those news cameras in the press room have your story, and they know your name. Most predators want easy prey. You are no longer easy prey."

I didn't realize it then, but I'd taken my first step that day to become a leader...a leader in a movement that would encourage others to speak out, and not be afraid. And I also established a new strategy for stalking victims, a technique I later dubbed Hiding in Plain Sight.

Hiding in Plain Sight

For those with a strong presence in the community, Hiding in Plain Sight provides an option to stay visible and connected in the community, while neutralizing the stalker. Over the next few years, I leveraged that initial TV appearance into dozens of interviews on TV as well as in magazines and newspapers. People recognized my face and knew my story. I began to write columns for the local newspapers and magazines as "guest commentary."

I used my skills working in real estate, the investigative field and in credit and collections, to write articles offering tips and tricks for overcoming identity theft for starters.

I made a name for myself in my community, my state, and across the country by speaking out on behalf of victims. I worked with law enforcement and lawmakers around the nation to change laws to protect those who were abused, stalked, or experiencing cyberstalking. My messages gradually took hold, and laws were passed to help others who were trapped as I had once been.

I continued to be cyberstalked and stalked, and at one point my cyberstalker tried to sue me for defamation of character. But the power had shifted. I set up an answering service and directed all messages that my cyberstalker sent via phone or email, to my ever-growing incident file and recorded them in my "Events Time Line."

Eventually, the messages tapered off, when the stalker realized I was unaffected by them. With law enforcement knowing his name and face, it was unlikely that he'd hurt me. If he did, everyone would know where to look.

Later, I helped an aspiring political candidate use this technique to free himself from the grip of a persistent stalker and cyberstalker. I encouraged Randy to do what I had done for the past few years...get his face and story out to the press.

Randy's Story

Randy had dated a woman for only a few months but had broken up with her. Lisa dreamed they'd marry, and she aspired to be a politician's wife, so she was unwilling to let him go. At first, her emails were pleas to get back together, but once Randy made it clear he was no longer interested in a relationship, her messages turned ugly.

Mud-Slinging

She wrote disparaging comments about him on Facebook and other social media sites, and took out ads in the newspaper, attacking his integrity and loyalty to the political party. She lied about things he'd done and portrayed him as a womanizer who slept with a different woman every night.

In his small Midwestern town, people were conservative, so her smear campaign was costing him his career. He was soon trailing far behind the other candidates. Lisa even followed him on the campaign trail and stood up in public meetings to challenge him, trying to damage his reputation.

At his wit's end and about to drop out of the race, Randy contacted SIA. I suggested that rather than trying to hide, he go public about the situation. The idea went against Randy's beliefs that he should appear strong and in control, but at this point, he had nothing to lose, so he took my advice and called a press conference.

Honesty Pays

He'd been expecting negative press following his announcement that he was stalked and cyberstalked. Instead, he was shocked at the groundswell of support. Reporters interviewed him about the situation. People picked apart Lisa's messages on Facebook and in the ads, many left supportive posts or pointed out flaws in her information. As the media dug deeper into the story, they tracked down Randy's colleagues, college professors, and others to get more information on Randy's activities and character.

Because he'd been planning on a political career since high school, his record was squeaky clean. As a high school class President and valedictorian, he was liked and admired, so his classmates had only good things to say about him.

Digging into his and Lisa's backgrounds, they discovered that Lisa had received a diagnosis as bipolar at sixteen. The news media kept Randy's name in the public consciousness throughout the campaign. His cyberabuser, her reputation, and credibility tore apart by the press, moved to another state to escape the notoriety. And it was no surprise to anyone, except Randy, when he won the election by a landslide.

Greater Threats

The hiding-in-plain-sight technique works well, particularly with stalkers who care about their reputations, are fearful of being caught, or can be hindered by public opinion. Some stalkers, though, care little what others think and are driven by rage so great that they'll stop at nothing to destroy their victims. They may have personality disorders or consumed by rage and the need to control, that they will even kill. Abusive spouses scorned lovers, or vengeful employees intend to make the victim pay, even at the cost of their lives. They're on a mission to kill and destroy; prison is no threat. If your stalker is in this category, you may fear for your life, if you escape. Identity change may be your only choice for survival.

Identity Change

Identity change is only considered in the most dangerous situations because a complete identity change means taking on a whole new identity. Choosing this method of escape is always a last resort, and you must be certain you're ready. You must leave behind everything you own and everyone you love to start a new life with a brand-new name, so it's usually only done to prevent homicide. This approach requires as much determination and passion as hiding in plain sight, but with the caveat that you will be starting over from scratch. If your life is at risk, though, it may be your only option.

Gideon's Story

Gideon, an art show director, evicted a woman from the apartment building he owned. Zoe was furious and cyber-stalked him. It began with hang-up calls, nasty emails, and rumors that he'd made sexual advances. Gideon ignored all of it, assuming it would soon go away on its own. Instead, it got worse, much worse.

Maniacal Stalker

Zoe tracked him via his art gallery's online calendar and traveled to every event to make his life miserable. She also hired private investigators to trail him and take pictures for her. Then one night, after an art opening, she shot him twice as he exited the gallery.

Gideon survived and testified against her, but the jury did not find her guilty of attempted murder. Instead, she was convicted only of stalking and misdemeanor, which meant she spent no time in jail. After the trial, she told the news media that she was the real victim and fabricated a story of his abuse, making him out to be the guilty party.

Increasing Danger

Zoe's emails and phone messages grew more irrational, as did her veiled threats indicated that she planned to finish the job this time. Going out in crowds and taking all the usual precautions for stalkers were no help for Gideon. He lived in fear, never knowing when she would strike again.

While he was recuperating, he read a magazine article about identity changes and contacted me. I helped him go underground with a changed name and social security number. Gideon sold his property, moved to another state, and had plastic surgery to change his appearance. He lost everything, including his career, his MFA degree, his credit rating, all his friends and art contacts. He can never contact his father or sister again, and he had to start over in a new job without prior experience or qualifications. He was willing to give up everything to stay alive.

So, too, was Skylar.

Skylar's Story

After enduring years of abuse, she fled. Skylar's ex-lover, a police officer, tracked her down wherever she went. He beat her up several times, twice badly enough that she had been hospitalized. But her ex's law enforcement buddies protected him and refused to take a report. Then one night her ex-lover grabbed her, dragged her into an alley, pulled a gun on her, and threatened to use it if she didn't return.

She complied and endured several more weeks of abuse as she worked with SIA to change her identity and get a Canadian visa. Once everything set into motion, she disappeared one day while he was at work, leaving behind all that she owned. She is now a Canadian citizen and works from home writing web copy and ads for businesses.

Life-Changing Decision

Identity change is a serious decision with far-reaching consequences. For those who have to leave family members behind, it can be a gut-wrenching decision. Making this choice means never seeing or contacting them again. It might mean not watching nieces and nephews grow up. It means not being present at your parents' deathbeds. It means never knowing if your best friend married or had a baby.

It means losing years of experience and training at a job and needing to start over at a menial level.

Everything from college to medical school degrees is wiped out in an instant. It means retaking driver's tests, having no credit rating, having no "next of kin" to fill in on applications. It means having no medical records, prescriptions, health insurance.

It is used only as a last resort. But if you must choose between losing your possessions or losing your life, an identity change is a homicide prevention tool.

Tips on Identity Change

Many victims who have utilized this approach are living abroad or in new locations within the United States. To change your identity requires the support of law enforcement, prosecutors, the Social Security Administration, advocates, and public officials.

Be aware that identity change is not foolproof. In this cyber-age, determined predators or skilled hackers may break into protected databases and government records. It's also possible that credit reports and other agencies may commingle records from your past and present, which can open you up to accusations of identity theft!

If the Social Security Administration (SSA) denies you a social security number change, citing "lack of ongoing abuse," appeal this decision by engaging with an attorney, your local law enforcement, prosecutors, political representatives, assembly member, and Senator.

Bring your documentation and seek their support in forwarding your application back to SSA along with their recommendation. The majority of abuse and stalking victims find that a social security number change gets denied on the first attempt. Don't be discouraged; continue to reapply and pursue your goal until you have the necessary tools you need to become a survivor.

Public Policy Changes Are Desperately Needed

The past 13 years I have actively been pursuing public policy changes. The Social Security Administration and the victim service providers have done little to nothing to address the needs of domestic violence, cyberabuse and stalking victims of today who are at high-risk for homicide.

I applied for a "Social Security Number Change for Safety" myself, 12 years ago and I received an automated response letter from Social Security Administration that stated that I was not granted a social security number change due to "lack of ongoing abuse." I was experiencing ongoing abuse, in fact, I reported nearly 100 incidents in a matter of months!

This roadblock in my safety and homicide prevention planning instilled upon me the desire to be an even stronger advocate for myself and others. I am determined to find ways to help high-risk stalking and domestic violence victims throughout the United States to overcome the pitfalls of the failing public policy and procedures in the areas of identity change and social security number change for safety.

Being a pioneer in this field and facing insurmountable odds myself as a victim now a survivor, has not been easy, to say the least. Truthfully, the pushback from public officials, policy makers, women's organizations, government-funded victim service providers, and the Social Security Administration amongst others has been difficult to handle. Their failure to address the issue of homicide prevention and updating the identity change program to meet the needs of victims in the 21st century has been the biggest challenge I have faced so far.

The consequences of the lack of response from the powers that be have lethal consequences. These are life or death consequences for millions every year. Therefore do nothing, for me, was and continues to be, NOT AN OPTION!

I have experienced nothing but push back, and even an idle threat from the US Office of Inspector General, claiming my volunteer work with Survivors in Action, helping victims of abuse was somehow illegal.

Holding steadfast to my promise to continue to never back down and to be silent no more, I enlisted the help of the ACLU California to come to my aid as well as the aid of Survivors in Action in response to a letter received from the US Inspector General. Since drafting and submitting the response by the ACLU to the Office, no further inquiry regarding my work or that of Survivors in Action has been called into question again.

However, the lack of response remains an obstacle for victims facing life or death. They are at high risk of homicide in our country. These victims remain without help and lack any direct support, and this must change.

On behalf of those experiencing cyberabuse, stalking and domestic violence, and labeled high-risk as they battle for their lives, as well as the victims lost to homicide, I shall continue to honor you and to continue my work.

"No victim should be left behind" and "No one should have to live or work in fear!"

CHAPTER 27

Dealing with Depression and Suicide

The emotional trauma of dealing with cyberstalking or stalking can leave you exhausted and depressed. So can the related problems of broken relationships, lost jobs, damaged reputations. Maybe you can't face another day of relentless bullying, cruel taunts, and terrorizing threats; maybe you've received messages telling you that you should die.

When you can't see any way out, sometimes suicide seems the only option. If you are considering suicide, please call or contact someone immediately. And take some time to read this chapter. Perhaps it will give you a glimmer of hope in the midst of your unbearable pain. Many people who experience stalking or cyberstalking think about taking their lives. I was one of those people. Today, I am a licensed attorney in California, but I was once a victim myself, so I know how it feels. What many people don't know is that when my life reached rock bottom, I chose to commit suicide. I couldn't go on. There was nothing left for me. I'd escaped the physical abuse, but couldn't endure the ongoing stalking and cyberstalking. The loss of jobs and friends, the terror of being hunted had taken its toll. I had no way out. Unless I took action, my life would remain in this downward spiral forever. The action I chose was to end it all.

My Suicide Attempt

After learning that my beloved grandmother was dying of cancer, I reached the darkest point in my life. I had no reason to keep living. When I fled my ex, I'd left behind my two dogs, my car and everything I held dear.

Since that time, the cyberabuse and stalking I had endured had cost me two jobs, destroyed my credit rating, cut off my utilities, and drained my bank account. I had no money to pay bills, and bill collectors, some brandishing guns, were hounding me day and night. I was in constant physical pain as well. I had sustained permanent nerve damage to the left side of my face. My face pounded and pulsated to the point that I had to lie down often. I developed terrible migraine headaches that made it impossible for me to stand, walk and to keep my balance. Sunlight and any light directed at my face caused me pain, and using the computer for long periods was nearly impossible for me. I was tired most of the time from enduring the pain in fact.

Other than my grandmother, everyone else had abandoned me. Friends and family wouldn't risk their lives to spend time with me. The lawyers I hired to fight for me quit. I received death threats, and I lived in constant fear. Alone and trapped in a never- ending nightmare, I could see no way out. Suicide seemed the only option.

To thwart my stalker, I had paid rent for a year, in advance, and in cash to live in an old run down two bedroom, two bath apartment, in exchange for the landlord not running my personal credit. The heater didn't work, and the place had been occupied by a smoker before I lived there. My clothing, skin and entire body reeked of cigarettes. It was agonizing.

I was sleeping in my clothes wearing a jogging suit and my tennis shoes to bed, and because it was so cold, I was wearing a knit stocking cap and could see my breath when I breathed. I shivered most nights to sleep if I slept at all. It was a crappy existence and one I do not wish upon anyone, not even my worst enemy.

I had gotten a job offer and realized after I accepted it, that it was a con, and it turned out to be the final blow that was going to be my knock-out punch.

Final Decision

The phone rang incessantly in the background, but I ignored it as I prepared to die. As I sat on my couch with a bottle of pills and some vodka, someone pounded on my door.

Again, I ignored it and unscrewed the cap on the pill bottle. Outside my bedroom window, a face appeared. A business colleague, aware of how despondent I'd been over my recent job loss, had panicked when he couldn't reach me by phone. Now he was signaling to me to let him in. When I didn't respond, he started removing the window screen. My plans interrupted, I let him in.

My rescuer sat beside me on the couch. He didn't do anything special, only listened without judgment. That was all I needed. After talking for hours, I realized I'd been about to give up my life for my stalker. That made me angry, and I was determined to do whatever I could to beat this predator rather than be his prey.

Once I made that decision, I never looked back. That simple decision set me on a path to a future that I could never have imagined. When I made a choice to overcome stalking and cyberstalking, I had no idea how I'd accomplish it. I still had nothing, no money, no job, nor resources. All I had was my determination.

Moving Forward

That proved to be enough. I had no idea that someday I'd be helping victims from around the world as a Risk Management Consultant and if anyone had told me that in a few years I'd be a sought-after speaker, expert, and attorney in California, I never would have believed them. At that time, I was terrified to leave my house or to go out in public. I had no idea that I'd soon be stepping onstage to speak to thousands of people, giving TV interviews, or contributing to magazines.

I focused on taking charge of my life. One step at a time, I fought my way free. I developed strategies that have helped thousands of other victims escape from abusers, stalkers, and cyberstalkers. And by telling my story, I have saved countless people from committing suicide. My message to anyone who only wants to end the pain is: Tell someone first.

Tell a trusted friend, a relative, a colleague, a neighbor. If there's no one you can trust, call a hotline. Don't hint around. Speak the truth; say what's on your heart. Talking saved my life, and it could save yours.

Seeds of Greatness

Most people only want the pain to end; they don't want to die. Your life is precious, and you have no idea what your future will hold. You may not see your potential or the gifts you will someday give the world, but others can.

Like me, you too have seeds of greatness buried in your life, although you may not realize it. I thought I had no future. But that awful moment in time when I'd reached my lowest point turned out to be my greatest asset.

Time of Darkness

You may have reached your lowest point, the winter of your soul. My passion for working in the landscape and outdoors helps me describe this best. Your seeds of greatness, are like seeds of all plants, they need time underground in the darkness before they germinate. Everything may appear bleak, but it is only part of the greater cycle of life.

That low point in my life allowed the seeds to sprout into what eventually became my greatest gift to the world. Deep inside you, a seed is buried. A seed that one day will become your greatest gift.
It may not feel like it now, but you and your life matter to others. If not in your present situation, they will be in the future. You may have more than you can cope with right now. Reaching this point doesn't mean there's something wrong with you. Perhaps you have no support, nowhere to turn, and the pain seems endless. Suicide will end the pain, but it also will end your precious life and that beautiful seed, your great potential, will be lost to the world.

The First Step

It may take courage, more courage than you believe you have right now, to reach out for help. But if you do, you will be giving the world a gift. If you don't believe this is true, imagine telling someone who loves you that you're about to commit suicide. How would your loved ones feel and what would their reaction be?

Your life is so important that if you told perfect strangers your intentions, they'd try to stop you from dying because your life matters. People have climbed out on ledges to talk down jumpers. They know the jumpers have much to offer the world.

And you do too. Someday you will look back on this moment and be glad you chose life.

Feeling Overwhelmed and Hopeless

Often cyberabuse and stalking reach the point that victims feel so much despair they lose all hope. They may feel they're alone in the world and that nobody cares. Some see themselves as a burden to others and think everyone would be better off if they were dead. Perhaps that's how you've been feeling.

At this moment, your life may not seem valuable or even worthwhile, but that's because you cannot see the future. You have no idea what your future holds. People who have reached the bottom have the greatest empathy for others and go on to do amazing things. Even if you can't believe this is possible in your situation, it can happen. In fact, quite a few famous authors, artists, inventors, and movie stars attempted suicide early in life. Think how much richer they made the world by choosing life.

Dealing with Humiliation

If you're feeling worthless and useless, ashamed and humiliated, get angry. Not at yourself, but at the people who have done this to you. Often that's enough to change your whole mindset. Determine not to let them win. If they do, they'll do it again and again. You have the power to stop them. If you can't do it on your own, call one of the self-help organizations. Let them take on the battle with you.
Or call me!

Rewire the Memories

Suppose you'd never read those messages, you didn't know they existed; you had no idea those pictures or videos had been posted. How would your life be different? Try journaling about these. Keeping the Events Time Line was powerful for me...it served the purpose of recording events and maintaining an evidentiary trail, and it also served as a therapeutic way to express what I was experiencing. It allowed me to release it so that I didn't have it inside of me growing like a tumor ready to explode.

Put the situation in perspective. Who are the people who are making your life miserable? Should they have the power to control your life? What have they done to deserve the right to hurt you? Are they better than you, especially deep down where it counts? Do you have to accept their assessments of you?

Project into the future. Five years from now, will anyone know who these bullies are? Will you even remember them or have any contact with them? Will these incidents still affect you? You never know where you'll be in the future. Someday you may be in a position to deny the bully something important, such as a job, a loan, or an autograph.

One movie star admitted that, while she was growing up, she was bullied mercilessly by a gang of girls who mocked her and had beaten her up in the school restroom. Years later after she was famous, she was in a restaurant when two of those bullies approached her for her autograph. Now the power was reversed, and she reminded them of what they'd once done to her. She could even choose to deny their request.

Change Your Posture

Shame results in physical reactions: curling up, averting the eyes, hiding. Even small children, when they feel ashamed, cannot meet someone's eyes, so they often run and hide. Embarrassment makes us want to pull the covers over our heads and hide.

Check your posture right now. Are you slumped, curled inward, hanging your head, biting your nails? Take the opposite position: stand up straight, shoulders back, head held high, looking straight ahead. Imagine meeting the person or group who's abusing you while you're in this position. See yourself meeting their eyes and saying, "I have nothing to be ashamed of; the one who should be ashamed is you." Practice claiming your power.

Stay in Present Time

Chances are, if you're reading this book, the cyberabuse or stalking isn't occurring right at this moment. Yes, your cyber-predator may be posting new messages right now, or your stalker may be trying to track you, but right at this moment in time, you're here, not there. With the computer turned off, the only place those messages, videos or photos exist is in your mind. If they're bringing you pain right now, it's because you're torturing yourself with the memories, imagining what others are thinking. Erase those thoughts from your mind by concentrating on the present.

Even if your cyberabuser sends ten messages in an hour, and they each take two minutes to read, in an hour, you'll have spent twenty minutes on them. What did you do with the other forty minutes? Worry about how many more messages the cyberpredator would send? Think negative thoughts about this person? Feel sick thinking about all the people who have seen the messages? Cringe in embarrassment?

Why not pull your forty minutes of attention away from the cyberabuse and use it for something that's important to you? Once you start doing this regularly, you'll reclaim huge blocks of time that you lost to negative thoughts. Count how many letters are on this page, or count your blessings, a challenge that can keep your mind occupied for a long time.

PTSD and Depression

Many victims of cyberabuse and stalking report an ongoing sense of terror, nervousness, sleep disturbances, fear of being alone or in dark places, jumpiness, and inability to relax. These symptoms often are associated with post-traumatic stress disorder (PTSD).

Although PTSD often is associated with returning military personnel, it can affect anyone who has been through a severe emotional trauma, particularly if it involved the threat of injury or death. Continual cyber-attacks have the same effect on the body and mind as physical threats; the constant fear and tension take a toll on both mind and body. Often these symptoms persist long after the situation ends.

Fight-or-Flight Response

As a victim, you live with trauma and fear. To combat the perceived danger, your body prepares to defend itself by flooding your system with chemicals so you can stay on high alert. Usually when adrenaline courses through the body in response to a dangerous situation, it provides a much-needed boost of energy, enabling you to run faster or fight harder to escape. Once the situation is over, your breathing calms, and your heart rate returns to normal. Gradually, the chemicals that allowed you to deal with the emergency dissipate, and your body relaxes.

If the attacks are ongoing, however, your body never goes back to normal. You remain in that state of high arousal, on constant alert, with fight-or-flight chemicals flooding your body continually.

Healing Power of Sleep

Sleep is one of the ways your body and mind process and heals traumatic experiences. If you are unable to sleep or are restless during the night, your brain has less time to work through the distress.　　Over time, lack of rest takes a major toll on your body. Negative emotions increase, causing the release of large amounts of stress hormones, leading to anxiety, depression, weight gain, digestive issues, and memory problems.　Stress also suppresses the immune system, making it more likely that you'll get ill. Lack of sleep also leads to depression.

Depression drains you physically, emotionally, and mentally, leaving you with little energy to act. You may feel listless and apathetic as if nothing matters. This lethargy often accompanies a sense of helplessness and hopelessness. Life seems overwhelming and difficult, and everything looks bleak.

The only choice I made when I decided against suicide was not to let the abuser win. If that's the only intention you have the strength to make, that's enough. You'll be astonished at how powerful that simple decision is. And if you don't even have enough strength to make that choice, dial the suicide hotline. Someone there can give you the support you need until you're able to decide.

Final Tips

- STOP! Do not take action if you are feeling suicidal. Give yourself a time limit, even if it's a day. During those twenty- four hours, you may change your mind. Keep returning to this step each day.
- CALL someone. Contact a friend, a neighbor, even a stranger. The suicide hotline, a counselor, clinic, or church, are options. Tell them what you plan to do, and tell them why. Listen to their advice.
- FORGIVE yourself. Be loving and gentle with yourself.
This pain was not your fault; you didn't deserve it. So
don't blame yourself. You deserve love and support, so

surround your- self with people who will give you what you need.

• VISUALIZE the future, a future without pain. Look for a ray of hope, for something positive you can or will do a few weeks or months from now.

When I was about to commit suicide, I couldn't see any story but the relentless pain, fear, and tragedy surrounding me. I envisioned it continuing forever and saw no means of escape. That tiny glimmer of hope, the decision to not give up lit the spark that later grew into a flame. Perhaps all you have left right now is a tiny ember, a small flicker of hope or anger or strength.

That's all it takes to set yourself free!

CHAPTER 28

Reporting to Law Enforcement   Creating the "Public Safety Paper Trail"

This chapter is written to acknowledge the fact that I always want victims to report to law enforcement but to do so knowing what is involved, and what this means so that you are not re-victimized when you do as so many are and as I was.

It discusses the civil suits against perpetrators (including re-victimizing by lawyers.)

It covers school regulatory reform (lots of cyberabuse is rampant on school campuses at all grade levels, and the school regulations are lax.)

I applaud Kathryn Warma, the US Attorney that helped me understand the difference between a legal advocate (what I am) a zealous advocate that has passion determination to help people and a lawyer a person with a law license that earns a paycheck.
Repeatedly throughout this book, I say to "Create the public Safety Paper Trail."

What I do not want for victims to do, however, is be re- victimized when they do. To prevent re-victimization which is why I am writing the book in the first place, I am explaining this in depth so that victims grasp that when you report, you must understand you are not reporting with the mindset that you will find help or that all of your problems will go away.

You are reporting because you need to document the activity so that an advocate will take you seriously whether it be me or another risk management consultant, attorney, public officials, a private investigator, a school official, prospective employer, a prospective spouse, you get the idea.

When you don't report, the public view is an immediate knee jerk reaction. Society will say, "If you didn't report, then you are somehow not a real victim." Or, "Obviously, if you didn't report it to law enforcement then you were not stalked or cyberstalked, and therefore you are a liar." Reporting is part of your recovery defense against further attacks but not for the reasons you may think before you read this book.

You cannot report believing that you will get help this will only hurt you, and second, you must understand that if you are taken seriously by law enforcement and prosecutors and the case is investigated, and there is an arrest the aftermath is not what you think.

The nightmare of living in fear and the online postings, videos, images, emails, text messages, nasty glares, emotional and financial loss and your entire world turned upside down will not be fixed by reporting to law enforcement. It just doesn't work that way.

First, you cannot think that if you garner an arrest, there will be a conviction. There may be nothing at the end. Possibly there is an arrest and a plea bargain resulting in no jail time and probation, or a payment of a fine. Or, it may be that there is an arrest, and later the charges are dropped. The third scenario is that there is an arrest, a jury trial, and the perpetrator is found not guilty.

Worse yet, when you report, and there is an arrest, at times this escalates the behavior, and it becomes a catalyst for the stalker to act out against you more - I know this personally.

I reported to law enforcement, they interviewed the perpetrator and immediately afterward the behavior the stalking and cyberstalking escalated – it was as if a fuse had been lit setting off a bomb, I mean this! Every time I reported, this happened, and because the predator was reading my emails he was excited and empowered to return fire on me even stronger than before!

Predators are not stupid. Many cyberabusers with whom I have discussed this topic with did their research ahead of time. They use the internet to stalk, have read and researched all about the ways it can be done and spend countless hours fine- tuning their craft before they commence the conduct. During and after cyberassaults or stalking episodes, they research to see what reaction they are having as I have discussed previously.

They are seeking a reaction because that is what they want. Law enforcement interviewing them is a reaction – and most understand that law enforcement has little power to do anything because of today's antiquated laws. They laugh and consider this part of the process. Predators know the worst case scenario is little to no jail time, perhaps probation or fines. They also know that law enforcement doesn't take cyberabuse or stalking seriously and they know exactly how far they can go before they are punished and what would happen when they are.

Most predators know the law better than any criminal defense attorney or prosecutor I know. They keep up on the current case law, follow the media reports and enjoy knowing that the predatory behavior will always outpace the antiquated laws and victim resources. Perhaps I say – or perhaps NOT.

I am not backing down. I now have a law license, and I have many ideas as to how the legislature and law enforcement can get up to speed quickly. I will do my best to ensure this happens! Laugh now, predators! It may not be so funny or fun in the future!

Punishment is insignificant

Not one predator I have spoken with the past 13 years has been afraid. Even after conviction, they stated that they felt no pain as far as the punishment goes. At times they express remorse. Some have said they were sorry and had written letters to the victims, but as far as the punishment fitting the crime or somehow inflicting any pain like what the victims go through that is not the case. Most of the predators laugh and say the punishment is a joke. I couldn't agree more. Understand this and do not get re- victimized. Many are.

Garnering a Criminal Conviction – Change the mindset or risk serious disappointment

Victims experiencing stalking and cyberabuse have no direct support to overcome the abuse. Your only line of defense other than the tips in this book is consulting with me directly, using attorneys, private investigators, and reporting to law enforcement.

To prevent being re-victimized, my goal is to help change your mindset in regards to reporting to law enforcement.
Report the incidents! It's in my steps and solutions, and it is listed where appropriate.

I had reported up and until I was told not to, thinking that I was going to get help. Once I realized no help was coming, my mindset shifted. I was reporting for evidentiary purpose ensuring if and when the predator attacked myself or someone else; there would be a history. If the predator had succeeded in killing me, he would be the first to be interviewed by detectives.

Before my change in mindset, I was already re-victimized. My grandmother and I thought that once we reported, the police would investigate, the predator would get arrested, and we'd have some peace. It was not a reality. Rather than expect and rely on this outcome, change your mindset.

Expect nothing other than creating an evidentiary trail for you to use, perhaps later in a civil case or if and when the predator strikes out big enough to garner the attention of law enforcement and prosecutors. The reports will be there because you have done your due diligence. This paper trail is also vital for private investigators, risk management consultants, (like me), and lawyers to be able to help you and for you to use as a tool to help restore your reputation as discussed above.

Cyberabuse and stalking cases are at best misdemeanor crimes in the majority of cases, if a crime at all. Read any news headline, and you will find the overall result – the punishment for the conduct is probation at best, along with small fines or probation itself in some cases. Predators do not consider this to be punishment. In my interviews and discussions on this topic with those convicted of stalking and cyberabuse, many told me point blank that the punishment is nothing and certainly not a deterrent. They thought it was laughable at best. Rather than falsely and naively believe that reporting is going to solve your problem, get you remedy or compensation or bring you "Justice," change your mindset. Reporting may never help in your case, but you are defending your rights to be free and standing up for yourself. If and when the perpetrator strikes at another, which they often do, your report will be there to build a much stronger case. You will have the report to utilize as a tool for overcoming the societal obstacles of today of explaining why you have the online reputation or other issues that are lots less explainable without it.

Again, don't report with the mindset that you are going to be set free from abuse or receive help. Don't believe that by reporting, somehow all of this misery and suffering is going to go away or be remedied. That kind of mindset will only hurt you in the long run because the majority of cases are neither prosecuted nor vigorously investigated. They are reports that sit in a database beside thousands of other cases.

The reality is that jails are overcrowded with violent criminals, murderers, rapists, etc. and cyberabuse is often a misdemeanor charge such as an invasion of privacy or similar charge rather than labeled what it is. Laws are antiquated and not up to date with the conduct of the cyberabuse predator.

Even After a Conviction Danger lurks - Cyberstalking from Inside Prison Walls

Since I began working with crime victims 13 years ago, growing numbers of cases involving cyberstalking from behind prison walls have been coming up. Particularly those charged with domestic violence or attempted murder that also had prior stalking and cyberstalking incidents. They end up going to prison for short periods of time, and using the electronic equipment including cell phones they have access to, and can stalk from behind prison walls. There is no guarantee this won't happen even when the predator is in jail. The same solution steps, mindset, and self- advocacy must continue.

Why Cases Are Not Investigated and Prosecuted

It takes diligence to investigate and prosecute a cyberabuse case. US Attorney Kathryn Warma in Washington State prosecuted the first cyberstalking case in the US long before cyberstalking became recognized as a crime. The Murphy case.

In this case, a brave victim persevered, garnering help by speaking out, and reporting the instances of cyberstalking to law enforcement. Because of the passionate prosecutor, US Attorney Kathyrn Warma, and a determined FBI agent, who was willing to spend thousands of hours investigating, this case had a happy outcome. Police took action, and the charges filed.

By applying the Federal Telecommunications Act to a cyberstalking case, (yes prosecutors can find ways to prosecute cyberabuse cases using existing laws, but this takes time and effort), led to the prosecution of the first case of cyberstalking. It resulted in a plea bargain and a misdemeanor conviction. The outcome fell way short of what it should have been. This reality of years ago continues to this day.

I am very fortunate I was able to speak with the US Attorney during my period of reporting instances of cyberstalking to law enforcement. In so doing, I was able to learn not expect any help, to stay the course, and to report to create a public safety trail and nothing more. My focus remained on my self-advocacy measures which were slowly taking hold and pursuing cyberstalking legislation and reform of victim resources.

What I learned here from the Murphy case was invaluable. The most important of all – it was up to me to protect myself. The chances of finding a legal advocate like US Attorney Warma in my state was nil. Finding someone willing to spend countless hours pursuing a legal case, taking a chance and filing charges for a case involving a new area of law, ("cyberstalking") using old antiquated existing laws were slim to none. Much less was the chance of finding an FBI agent or detective willing to back me. It was not going to happen for me and is not a reality for the majority of victims.

I gained the powerful insight I needed to understand how powerful I could be by becoming an attorney advocate to provide others with "Moore Justice." I could use my passion like U

Attorney Warma coupled with creativity and help other victims and person's experiencing abuse of any kind by applying existing law to their situations until I could lobby the legislature to enact new laws. I understood that there were few if any attorney advocates like US Attorney Warma and that I would have to join in and take action or millions of victims were going to be left behind in perpetuity.

Moral of This Story: Report, Report, Report!

Report, document, put your guard up and use the tools in this book. Don't be naïve and think for a second you will have the support you so deserve from law enforcement or prosecutors. They are not prepared to help you or guide you out of the mess you are in, they clock in and clock out.

Police officers take reports, forward the police reports on for approval for investigation, or send the reports to the slush pile where they sit, and sit, and sit. If they do make it to the prosecutor's desk, they get a quick glance. If it's not an easy win, meaning "it's too complex of a case" or, there is no public outcry for the prosecutor, city attorney or district attorney to prosecute it will be passed over as part of the assembly line justice we have in America.

Time is the enemy for victims of cyberabuse and stalking as these cases take lots of time, and the reward is very little in comparison to the hours involved investigating by law enforcement and prosecutors prosecuting. Thousands of hours in exchange for nothing except perhaps being thanked publicly by the victim or their families. Perhaps they get a letter or notice of thanks at a press conference by public officials. The perpetrator is back on the street, most likely doing what they were doing before being arrested, and the cycle begins all over again.

I am not blaming any particular entity. Not police, prosecutors, etc. What I am stating is the facts. We need better laws so that we can ensure that the cases get taken seriously. The punishment has to fit the crime. Realistically, the punishment has to fit the time spent by law enforcement, and prosecutors or the victims will continue to be left behind with the predators prevailing... over and over. Here is the true essence of the problem we face.

Self-Advocacy is Key

Be proactive. Never let your guard down. Do not stop reporting, as this is the only defense mechanism available to our civilized society to prevent predatory conduct.

The feeling I had when the sheriff deputy said to stop reporting was devastating for my grandmother and me. We were relying on this help, this we thought was the magic weapon that was going to stop the abuse. Recognize that reporting is simply a tool in your toolkit. It is you that is the magic weapon. It is you that has the power to overcome and defend against the attacks. So change up the mindset protect yourself- see this reality first so that you are not devastated and fall to the low spot that I did.

Cyberabuse Regulation in Schools

School regulations are lax when cyberabuse reports are submitted. Far too often the outcome that the predator remains unaffected, returning to school as if nothing happened.

School regulations must evolve so that they address cyberabuse and they must classify cyberabuse as the heinous conduct that it is, just as they do acts of violence. If not, it will only continue, it will be a catalyst for why cyberabuse continues to escalate.

Speaking Out is Vital

Speak out to school officials, employers, employees, law enforcement, prosecutors, and public officials. If we don't speak out against it and say we are not going to tolerate cyberabuse in a civilized society and we want our laws to reflect it and our school regulations and employment regulations to include this conduct nothing will change.

Mindset of Reporting

Be aware of why you are reporting. Understand the potential outcomes. First and foremost know that reporting won't fix your pain, but it is the first step of you being able to overcome and attack as well as garner the support you need from friends, family, coworkers, classmates, and from society as a whole. It's a vital step, but the purpose is not what you may have thought or believed. That is why I am explaining in such vivid detail.

The pain I felt when I reported and was told "I was Crazy" was devastating. Even worse was the pain I felt understanding that even if they were to make an arrest, and convict that the charge would be only a misdemeanor, and little jail time if any. There was no guarantee that there would be a conviction and no getting back all of the time I lost advocating and fighting back, losing my grandmother along the way. None of this was going to be "compensated" or somehow rectified by my reporting to law enforcement or garnering a conviction.

The process of reporting is meant to create a public safety paper trail, and that is it. If you get a conviction, so be it. If you don't, so be it too. The goal is that you have done all you can to fight back and defend against further attack and if someone asks you including your friends, family or future generations. You can tell them what you did, and help to use it as a method to overcome any damage it has left online or offline.

Civil Remedies – A Jury Verdict is Just a Piece of Paper

I am an Attorney licensed by the State of California. I am a litigator and understand the court system and how civil judgments can be effective in helping victims of stalking and cyberabuse. I also know the judicial system has an ugly side.

Judicial Systems Ugly Side - Lawyers Using Victims as "Fame for Gain."

(Information on civil suits most lawyers don't tell you!)

I use the judicial system to help people, but the judicial system has its mean ugly side. My colleagues with law licenses often neglect to tell you the client what the dark side may be when pursuing a civil or a criminal case.

I read news headlines and cringe when it says 23 million dollar verdict against John Doe by Powerhouse Law Firm avenging a cyberabuse victim or any person for that matter. My first thoughts are – who is John Doe? Has he bankrupted already? And those poor people!

My background working in the debt collection industry, and as a high-tech investigator, locating people and assets for a living makes me a much better legal advocate. I understand the shortcomings of civil suits and that the jury verdict or judgment that says $24 million dollars may be nothing more than kindling for the next backyard bonfire.

Many lawyers take a civil case – cyberabuse or any case for the money, and far too often for the notoriety. The lawyers and law firms use the victim as a pawn in their "game for fame" so to speak. They put on the dog and pony show, filing a highly publicized civil suit against a perpetrator now defendant, to enlist the media exposure and public attention. They then take the case to trial, and the jury verdict comes back for however many millions of dollars. Everyone is cheering and having a ticker tape parade!

Everyone is cheering but the victim – that is right the victim is not cheering. In fact, the victim is now re-victimized yet again by the system they believed was there to help and protect them.

Here's Why

Defendant predators are not insurance companies or slot machines. The lawyers never told the victim how awful it is to go through a jury trial or any trial for that matter especially those cases involving non-consensual pornography, cyberstalking and stalking. The victim has to interface with the perpetrator or perpetrators and see them, be in the same room as them – hear them and get the glares and stares and the middle fingers and the "I will kill you bitch" mouthed at you as I did when you take the stand.

You will also have to endure the most grueling cross-examination from the defense attorney. Even if you were prepared for this, it is deep soul cutting shit that tears up your insides. Worse yet, you are truly never prepared for the feeling, and it never goes away entirely.

In my court experiences, I felt good quite frankly, because even with the lawyers next to me it was me who did all the talking. It was me who scribbled on the yellow legal notepad, what the lawyers should say. It was me who took the stand when I got my permanent domestic violence restraining order issued and got the judge to rule in my favor. I felt good because it was therapy for me to stand up to my predator in court –and to tell the world that I was sick and tired of being a victim and I demanded "Moore Justice."

I didn't mind the threats or the fear because I was already living in fear and threatened every single day. They had become part of my normal.

Better Yet, I Knew the Outcome!

I knew I would never collect a dime from the predator. He was judgment proof. I understood that the prosecutors and law enforcement were not going to help me and that whatever I was able to do myself in court was better than nothing. So by knowing this outcome ahead of time, before I walked through the courthouse doors and on through the metal detectors and in through the wooden doors leading into the courtroom, I understood what was in front of me, what the outcome would be and I was informed and prepared for it all.

Most victims are not prepared or aware of the potential outcomes. That's why I wrote the book and became a "Attorney Advocate". I can't sit idle and watch as victims fall prey to a broken system. If I save one person from this fate, that is better than doing nothing at all.

For all of the victims who may not be so informed, the bad news is lawyers will prey on you. They will seek the glory to take your civil case and pursue what they are claiming is justice against the predator on your behalf, but neglect to tell you that the predator can bankrupt the suit as soon as the judgment is entered. They can turn around after you the victim takes that beating on the stand and speaks out so bravely as you do and then poof all of that is for not – you won't recoup a dime. It is truly this way. Know this potential outcome that way you are not easy prey for lawyers or for any predator for that matter.

What I propose is you decide what is best for you. No lawyer can guarantee the outcome of your case no matter how wealthy the defendant may be, or what facts and laws you have on your side. The law is what I call that "fickle friend," and my law professor said it best to help me stay in law school when I realized how truly difficult it would be for me to help be the legal advocate I so wanted to be.

He said, "No argument is a weaker or a stronger argument, it is up to the judge and jury to decide." It's true, and I would like to add in that you make your own justice. I made "Moore Justice" happen because I refused to be a victim. I refused to allow another human being to take any more time away from me and I refused to be a bystander and watch as others fell victim to the same experiences as I did.

I sat idle long enough with lawyer after lawyer by my side and by the side of other victims, as a victims' advocate with Survivors In Action to understand that the lawyers were not legal advocates. They were lawyers. Lawyers are those who get a law license and practice law for money. It is their job – their 8 to 5.

A legal advocate is different. We pursue the law from the perspective that we are problem solvers. We want our clients to have a voice and to have the strongest advocate by their side possible. We don't want them to be silenced by a situation. Instead, we want their voices heard – we are the voice for those without one.

We don't allow politics or legal-ease to get in the way of the fact that there is a wrong that has been committed that should be made right. We explain that we cannot guarantee the outcome of any case or situation, but we understand and are here to be the best advocate we can be so that the client has a voice.

US Attorney Warma is a legal advocate! She is one reason why I stayed the course and pursued my California law license so vigorously. I realized as a cyberstalking victim, I owed her a debt of gratitude and that I could honor her work by becoming a legal advocate myself. This way, I would be a force for positive social change.

Keep in mind though, that in California alone there are over 200K licensed lawyers and very few legal advocates. This remains true across the nation and around the world. Protect yourself.

Be on guard to protect yourself from re-victimization. Ask questions and never be afraid to say NO. Your survival and your journey to justice - is your own. No one is walking that path with you - only beside you. So do what is best for you. Feel no guilt in making your own justice.

My path was to create "Moore Justice" a new kind of legal advocacy and become a risk management consultant and expert witness for others to utilize when they hit rock bottom or needed that voice to speak for them.

Make your own justice and have no regrets!

Appendix

Alexis Moore Attorney • Author • Advocate
www.alexismoore.com add www.consultwithalexismoore.com

The Events Time Line

		Stalking & Cyberstalking Events Time Line & Incident Report				
Date	Time	Incident Description	Location • Virtual Physical Contact	Witness Name Address/Phone	Police / Agency Report or Incident #	Officer Name Badge #

Go to: http://consultwithalexismoore.com/book/ to receive our
Events Time Line

CyberActive Services - Janita Docherty
www.cyberactiveservices.com.au

Survivors In Action, Inc.
www.SurvivorsInAction.org

PAGE INTENTIONALLY LEFT BLANK

PAGE INTENTIONALLY LEFT BLANK

PAGE INTENTIONALLY LEFT BLANK

PAGE INTENTIONALLY LEFT BLANK

PAGE INTENTIONALLY LEFT BLANK

PAGE INTENTIONALLY LEFT BLANK

PAGE INTENTIONALLY LEFT BLANK

PAGE INTENTIONALLY LEFT BLANK

PAGE INTENTIONALLY LEFT BLANK

PAGE INTENTIONALLY LEFT BLANK

Made in United States
North Haven, CT
14 November 2023

44020190R00124